Conten

GW00580017

The 10 walks

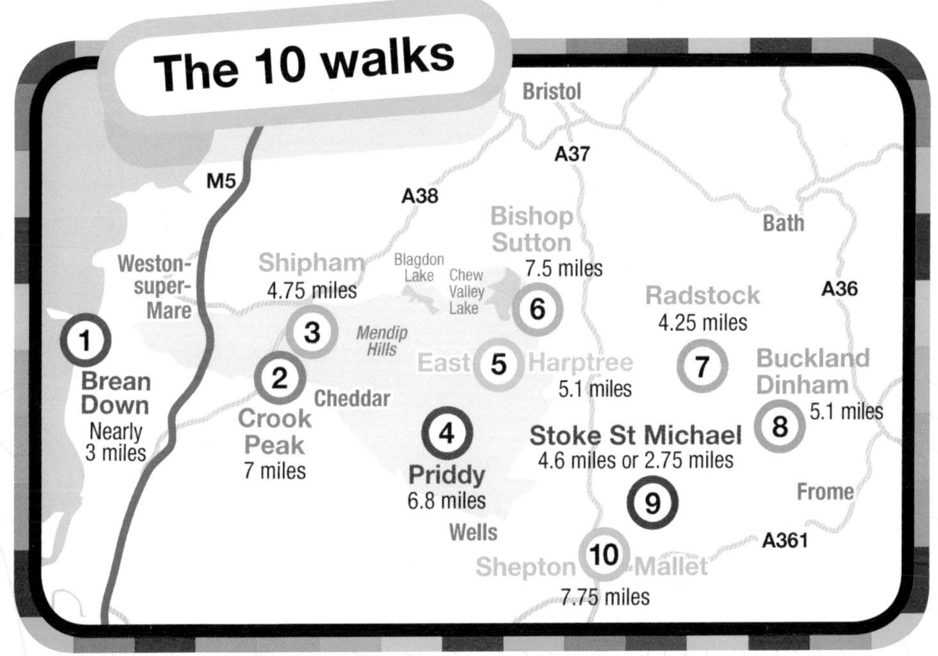

Bristol
A37
M5
A38
Bishop Sutton
7.5 miles
Bath
Weston-super-Mare
Shipham
4.75 miles
Blagdon Lake
Chew Valley Lake
A36
Radstock
4.25 miles
Mendip Hills
East Harptree
5.1 miles
Buckland Dinham
5.1 miles
Brean Down
Nearly 3 miles
Cheddar
Crook Peak
7 miles
Stoke St Michael
4.6 miles or 2.75 miles
Priddy
6.8 miles
Frome
Wells
A361
Shepton Mallet
7.75 miles

Introduction

The story of the Mendip Hills began some 416 million years ago during the Devonian period of earth's evolution, and it has been changing ever since. Mendip is very much a story of human impact on the landscape.

We all think of the natural environment being shaped by massive earth forces together with the erosive power of wind, water and sun. This is to a greater extent true, for it is the massive upheaval that shaped Mendip.

It is the exploitation of Mendip that has provided another story. Initially humans had little affect upon the surroundings in which they lived and died. Gradually however as the hunter gatherers settled down to farming some 4-5000 years BC they began to alter their surroundings to suit their needs. This process continues today.

The countryside is changing as our demands on it change and we are having an impact upon our environment such as never before. Farming is no longer the largest producer in a rural economy. It is however the creator of much of our heritage and the maintainer of our survival; there is much to see of our agricultural past on Mendip. But not everyone who lives in a village these days drives a tractor.

Mineral extraction of all types, from stone to lead, has scarred the earth. Lead is no longer dug from the Hill, but the evidence of centuries of extraction is all around. Quarrying is still an industry and draws its critics, but at the end of the day we all need stone in some form or another, and it's surprising just where it turns up.

"Miles More Mendip" is a walk book with a difference. It is not just about the miles covered and the views experienced, it is also about unlocking the landscape and discovering what lies beneath. It is a story which we hope will let you look upon this landscape with fresh eyes.

We hope that you enjoy the walks we have chosen to go into this book, and we also hope that Mendip will 'grip' you with an enthusiasm to go and find out more about the Hill.... It did just that for us! And our thanks to Chris Walters who checked many of the walks.

Brean Down
walk

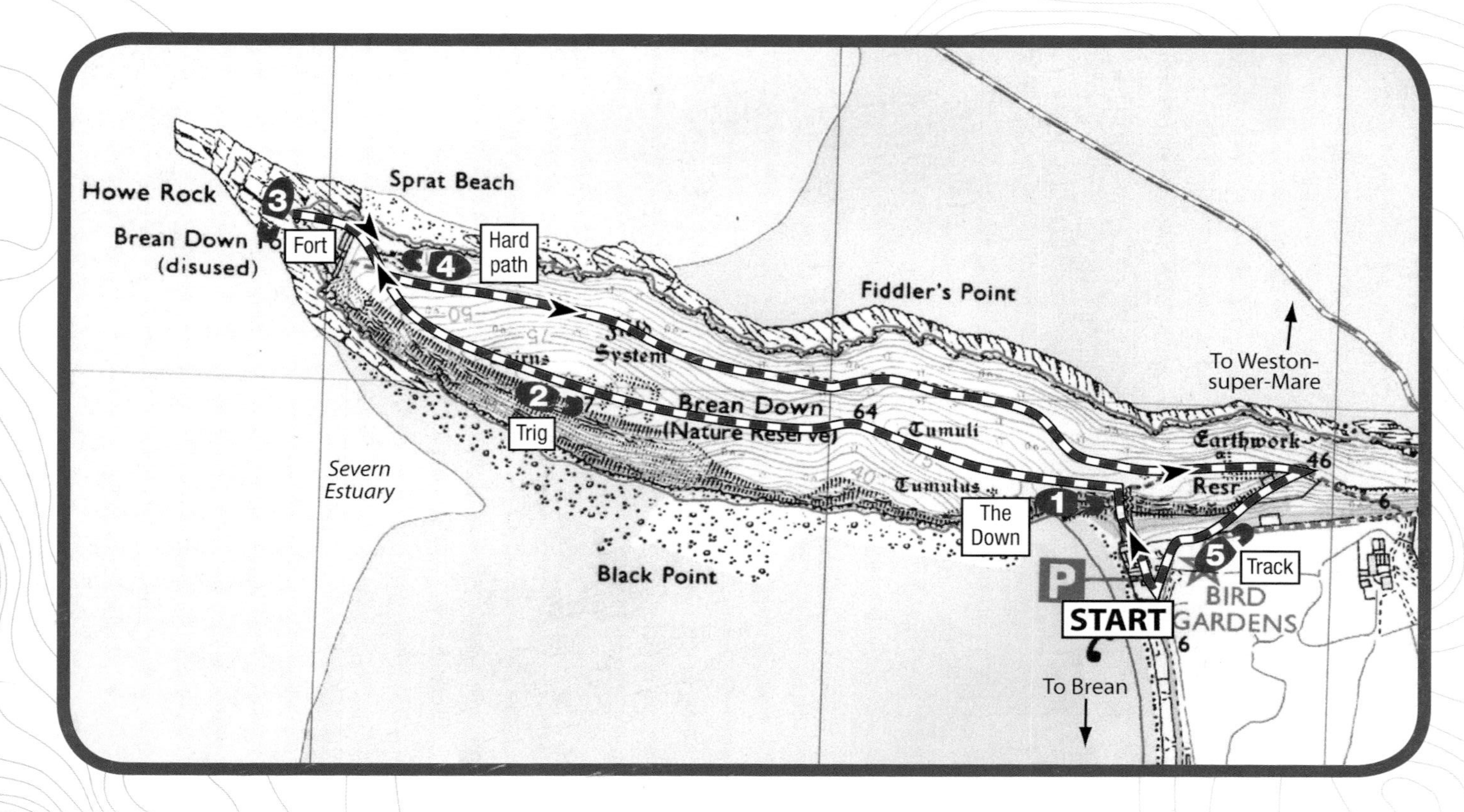
Howe Rock
Sprat Beach
(disused)
Fort
Hard path
Fiddler's Point
System
To Weston-super-Mare
Brean Down
(Nature Reserve)
Trig
Tumuli
Earthwork
Severn Estuary
Tumulus
Resr
The Down
Black Point
Track
BIRD GARDENS
START
To Brean

Brean Down walk

The 'giant whale' of the National Trust's Brean Down is the most westerly end of the Mendip Hills extending into the Severn Estuary. Find remains of an Iron Age hillfort and a Palmerston fort at the end used in the last War. Enjoy panoramic views. There are wild flowers in the limestone grassland, as well as sea birds.

It is a fascinating short circle starting strenuously with over 200 steps! There are cafes at the start and toilets. It can be very windy and exposed so go well prepared. You will need to keep your dog under close control.

MAP: OS Explorer 153 Weston-super-Mare & Bleadon Hill

GRID REF: 296 585

DISTANCE: Nearly 3 miles

TIME: About 2.5 hours walking; this allows time to look round the fort and elsewhere.

PARK: At the National Trust (NT) car park at the end of the Brean Down road (free for members, £3.40 a day non-members) or a few yards on in the Bird Garden car park, £2 for 4 hours. It is easy to access from J22 M5. Head for Burnham and then all the way up the coast road through Berrow and Brean to the end at Brean Down. Or from Brent Knoll and Lympsham you can cut across to the coast road.

Looking along the Down

START: Head towards The Down and then begin the steep stepped climb up to the top. Take your time and enjoy the views as you go. The Down is 1.5 miles long.

THE DOWN

Turn left and head out towards the end over the downland. You are following in the steps of man since the late Bronze Age when it was first occupied.

Pass ancient field systems on the way although they are virtually impossible to see. Human occupation dates back to the Beaker culture of the late Bronze Age. There is also evidence of an Iron Age hill fort and prehistoric barrows. There is evidence of a shrine dating from pre-Roman times which was re-established as a Romano-Celtic Temple in the mid c4th century. Several Roman finds including gold and silver coins Vespasian and a Roman carnelian ring were found at the site during quarrying.

The cliffs on the northern and southern flanks of Brean Down have large quantities of fossils laid down in the marine deposits about 320–350 million years ago.

The Down is now owned by the National Trust, and is rich in wildlife, history and archaeology. It is a Site of Special Scientific Interest due to both the geology and presence of nationally rare plants. It has also been scheduled as an ancient monument.

Brean Down

TRIG

You climb very gently and eventually reach the trig point. The 360° views from here are superb – across to Weston-super-Mare to Sand Point, Clevedon and the M5; over the Bristol Channel to the Brecon Beacons, Newport and Cardiff and out towards Port Talbot; Flat Holm and Steep Holm in the foreground, before sweeping over to Exmoor, with Dunkery Beacon visible; then back to the Quantocks and Hinkley Point, Bridgwater Bay and the Somerset Levels, Glastonbury Tor, Brent Knoll and Crook Peak.

You can look across the Channel to Lavernock Point.

In 1897, following wireless transmissions from Lavernock Point and Flat Holm, Guglielmo Marconi moved his equipment to Brean Down and set a new distance record of 14 kilometres (8.7 miles) for wireless transmission over open sea.

Going back over a century there have been plans for a tidal barrage from Brean Down to Lavernock Point. Nothing has come of these so far although further proposals may be put forward.

Continue on and start to drop down. You think you are about to go over the edge but then see the headland below and the spectacular sight of the Palmerston Fort.

It was built in 1865 as part of a chain of fort defences against possible French invasion, which in the event, never came. The fort was staffed by 50 officers and men of the Coast Brigade, Royal Artillery, but no shots were ever fired in action.

The end of the fort's active service came at 5 a.m. on 6 July 1900 when the No. 3 magazine which held 3 tons of gunpowder exploded after it was ignited by gunner Haines. No one knows why he did it, but it may have been an act of suicide.

It was then used as a café, owned by the Hillman family from at least 1907 until sold in 1936 to the 'bird sanctuary people'.

In the Second World War it again came into play as you will soon see. ➤

FORT

Cross the wide entrance ditch. Go into the fort and good labelling with excellent illustrations on many of the buildings help to give a good idea of the activity here.

On the outbreak of World War II, the fort was rearmed with two 6-inch (15-centimetre) ex-naval guns, and machine gun posts were built on the Down. Birnbeck Pier was taken over by the Admiralty in 1941 for weapon development. It was commissioned as HMS Birnbeck, and was used for secret weapons development and storage. The "Bouncing Bomb" was tested at Brean Down Fort.

Several other associated structures, including searchlight batteries for illuminating seaborne targets, a command post and the garrison barracks were built outside the original Palmerston fort. You can still see the bases of much of this.

The site was manned by 365 and 366 Coast Batteries RA of 571 Coast Regiment in 1942.

HARD PATH

Turn back and follow the main tarmac/stone track.

On your left was the site of a planned deep-water harbour. In the 1860s the aim was that this harbour would replace Bristol as a port for sailings to America and the export of minerals and agricultural produce.The foundation stones were laid, but the project was abandoned after a large storm.

As you proceed you can easily see the direction of the prevailing wind by the bent trees! There are wild flowers hugging the down - one of the rarest is the white rock rose. In Spring it is carpeted with bluebells.

TRACK

If you want to return via the steps,fork up right on the wide grass path, but if not, continue on the hard track which then bends right and drops down gently to the track at the foot of The Down. Turn right back to the start.

Palmerston Fort

Crook Peak
walk

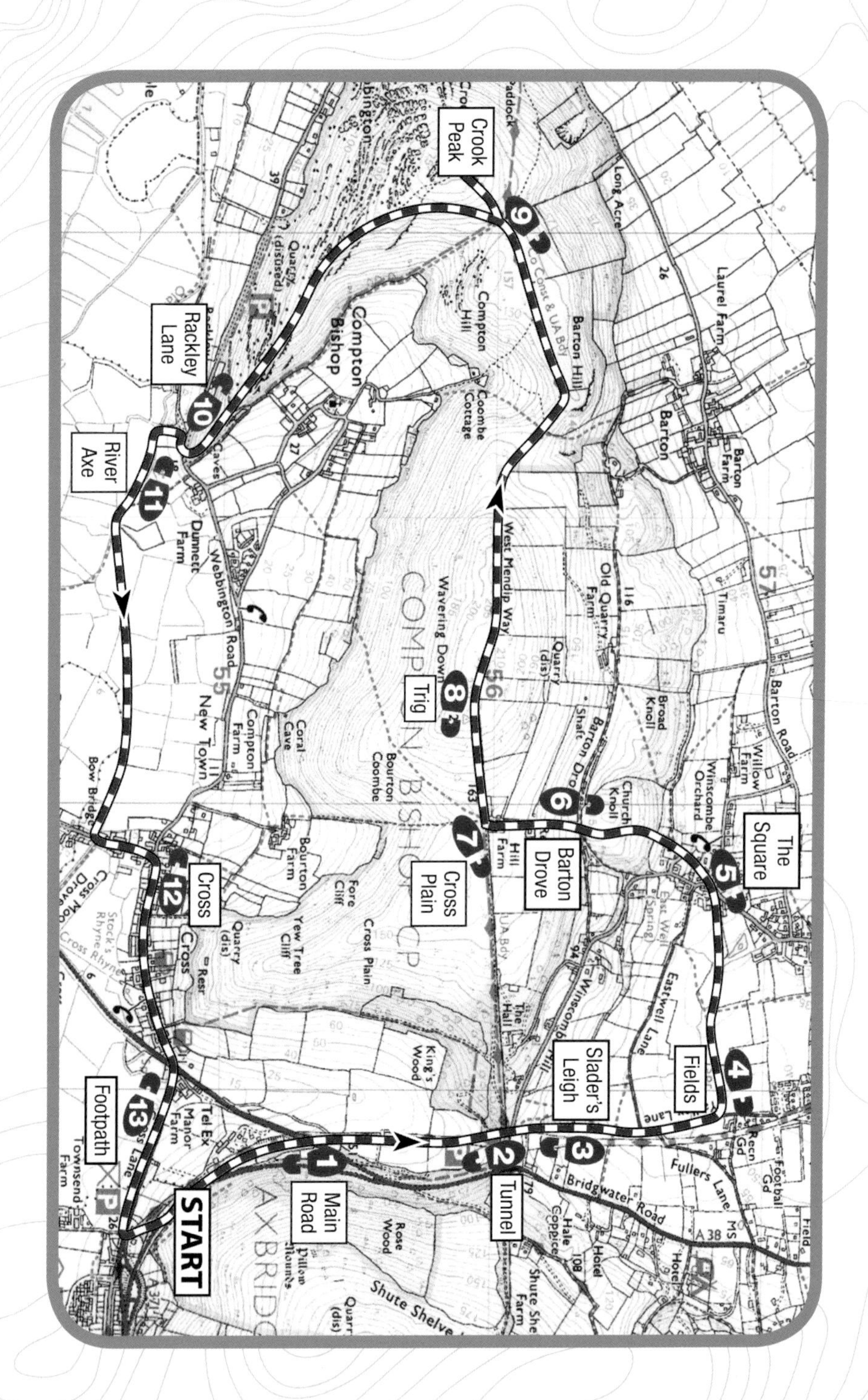
START
Main Road
Tunnel
Slader's Leigh
Fields
The Square
Barton Drove
Cross Plain
Trig
Crook Peak
Rackley Lane
River Axe
Cross
Footpath
Compton Bishop
West Mendip Way
Barton
Barton Road
Webbington Road
Winscombe Orchard
Bridgwater Road
Shute Shelve
Axbridge
Compton Hill
Wavering Down
King's Wood
Rose Wood
Dunnett Farm
New Town
Laurel Farm
Long Acre
Barton Hill
Broad Knoll
Church Knoll
Old Quarry Farm
Hill Farm
Bourton Farm
Bourton Coombe
Coral Cave
Compton Farm
Coombe Cottage
Bow Bridge
Fore Cliff
Yew Tree Cliff
Townsend Farm
Manor Farm
Eastwell Lane
Fullers Lane
Timaru
Willow Farm

Crook Peak walk

A fairly challenging circle of contrasts, best in good weather, this takes you on a different route up to Wavering Down and Crook Peak, the only pointed hill on Mendip. This is a prime summer ramble where flowers and bird life should be in abundance, and the views spectacular on a clear day. It begins along the old Strawberry Railway, across fields and up through a welcoming church in the old part of Winscombe. The climb towards Crook Peak goes up in stages and is not too difficult, although steep in places. The option is to climb to the top. Drop down a grassy ridge and follow the River Axe back to Cross village, with two pubs, and it's a short hop from there back to the start.

MAP: OS Explorer 141 Cheddar Gorge & Mendip Hills West

GRID REF: 423 548

DISTANCE: 7 miles

TIME: About 4 hours

PARK: In a free large parking lay-by to the west of Axbridge on the A371, a short distance from the A38. From the A38, coming South, cross the Somerset border and bear left towards Wells, Axbridge and Cheddar on the A371. Lay-by is half a mile on the right.

View from the ridge

START: Leave on the tarmac path near the car park entrance. Cross a side road and continue on the Cheddar Valley railway path along the route of the old Strawberry Line.

Opened in 1869 linking Yatton and Cheddar and Wells. it ran for nearly a century. Its most famous 'passengers' were the early strawberries from the Cheddar area sent up to Bristol by train and on to other markets – hence its nickname.

MAIN ROAD

At the A38 cross using the island and continue on the other side all the way to Shute Shelve Tunnel ignoring side turns.

TUNNEL

The 165 metre tunnel was blasted out of solid rock in 1868.

Go through. You can see the other end so it is not too dark and there should be solar lights down the centre. Out the other end pass an old wooden barrow and spade marking the start of digging of the Strawberry Line.

SLADER'S LEIGH

Keep on for a couple of minutes to steps up left and a sign for Slader's Leigh Nature Reserve. Go up the steps, across a crossing higher path and into the sheltered meadow which is owned and managed by the Mendip Society. In season it is full of wild flowers, butterflies and insects. There is a bench along the bottom if you want to stop for a while.

FIELDS

Go back out the gate, and immediately left along the upper path. At a crossing path by a Slader's Leigh Wheelchair Access sign go left into a meadow. Go straight across to a hidden stile opposite. Cross, go over a track, over another stile and turn right along the next field. Leave by a metal gate onto Eastwell Lane... often very wet and boggy and so to be avoided. Go straight over into the field and on to the end. See the splendid tower of Winscombe church over left.

Cross a footbridge and then bear diagonally left through the field. In the field, fork ➤

◀ Shute Shelve tunnel

left so that you go through a wide opening. Then go straight across the next field. Cross a small stream on stones. Maintain direction and cross a wooden footbridge hidden near the far right corner. Carry on along the right edge. Cross a stile to the right of a barn and a path leads on, through a yard and out to the road in old Winscombe.

THE SQUARE

Left a few yards is the Square. Go up Church Lane and continue to the steps to the c13th church.

St James is extremely welcoming – providing free coffee/tea for visitors. Among its delights are the stained glass windows and the carved angels round the edge of the barrel roof. Its 100ft high Perpendicular tower is one of the finest in Somerset.

To continue, go out the door and left round the side of the church and shortly bear up across the grass to the marked footpath and fixed kissing gate. Climb straight up the field and enter woodland over a stile. Go ahead a yard or two and then bear left up the stepped path. Continue steeply up, go through a gate and then level out in the open and head across a field.

BARTON DROVE

Reach a crossing track, Barton Drove, one of the old drover routes for moving animals across Mendip. Go more or less straight over on a tarmac path which climbs all the way up to Hill Farm and then through to Cross Plain (NT).

CROSS PLAIN

Turn right following the West Mendip Way.

The field wall right has been a boundary since Saxon times and it currently marks the boundary between Somerset and North Somerset.

St James, c13th church

Dry stone wall along the West Mendip Way

➤ Climb quite steeply to the Trig Point on Wavering Down at 211 metres – a little higher than Crook Peak itself.

TRIG

You are rewarded with spectacular views all round. Carry on following the West Mendip Way by the dry stone wall where volunteers have worked tirelessly for years. Drop downhill and continue by the wall.

CROOK PEAK

At the wall corner and a signpost reach the bottom of Crook Peak.

This name is believed to derive from the Saxon of 'cruc' meaning hilltop.

It is well worth going up the top if you want some sweeping views. Or stay on the path round the left side (ignore a footpath which drops down left). Climb and then reach a ridge and continue down this round the other side of the bowl, where the village of Compton Bishop nestles. There are good views across the Levels on the right. The ridge narrows. Stay with it all the way, going through a fence line and on ignoring side paths. Go straight ➤

➤ on down quite steeply passing alongside an old quarry. Reach a gate leading onto the road.

Cross with care on this difficult corner.

RACKLEY LANE

Rackley was a port on the River Axe in Roman times. However, today it is no longer navigable. Go down Rackley Lane, past a house, and then turn left through a gate on the track marked with a footpath arrow. Cross a bridge over the River Axe and immediately turn left over a stile by a gate.

RIVER AXE

The name is a version of a Saxon word for water. This flows from under the Mendip Hills rising at Wookey Hole where it is estimated to flow at around 33 million gallons of water (just over 15 million litres) a day and continues to Uphill.

Follow the Axe on your left all the way through fields for nearly a mile. Come out on a side road in Cross.

CROSS

Cross left over the stone bridge and continue to the Old Coach Road.

Turn right past an interesting variety of houses including one with great topiary. Reach the White Hart, an old coaching inn, and carry on further to the second popular Cross pub, the New Inn, serving food all day.

Reach the main A38 and cross to the road opposite leading to Axbridge, Wells and Cheddar. Use the grass verge on the right and after a couple of minutes take the marked footpath on the right through a gate by Springs Farm.

FOOTPATH

This parallels the road, behind a hedge, and comes out onto the road again at the far end. Cross the road and go up the lane opposite, be careful along here and cross to the far side. Shortly, just by a road sign, go up right on a small path and up steps through woodland to reach the parking and picnic area. Turn left back to the start.

The White Hart Inn, Cross
01934 732260

The New Inn, Cross
01934 732455

Shipham
walk

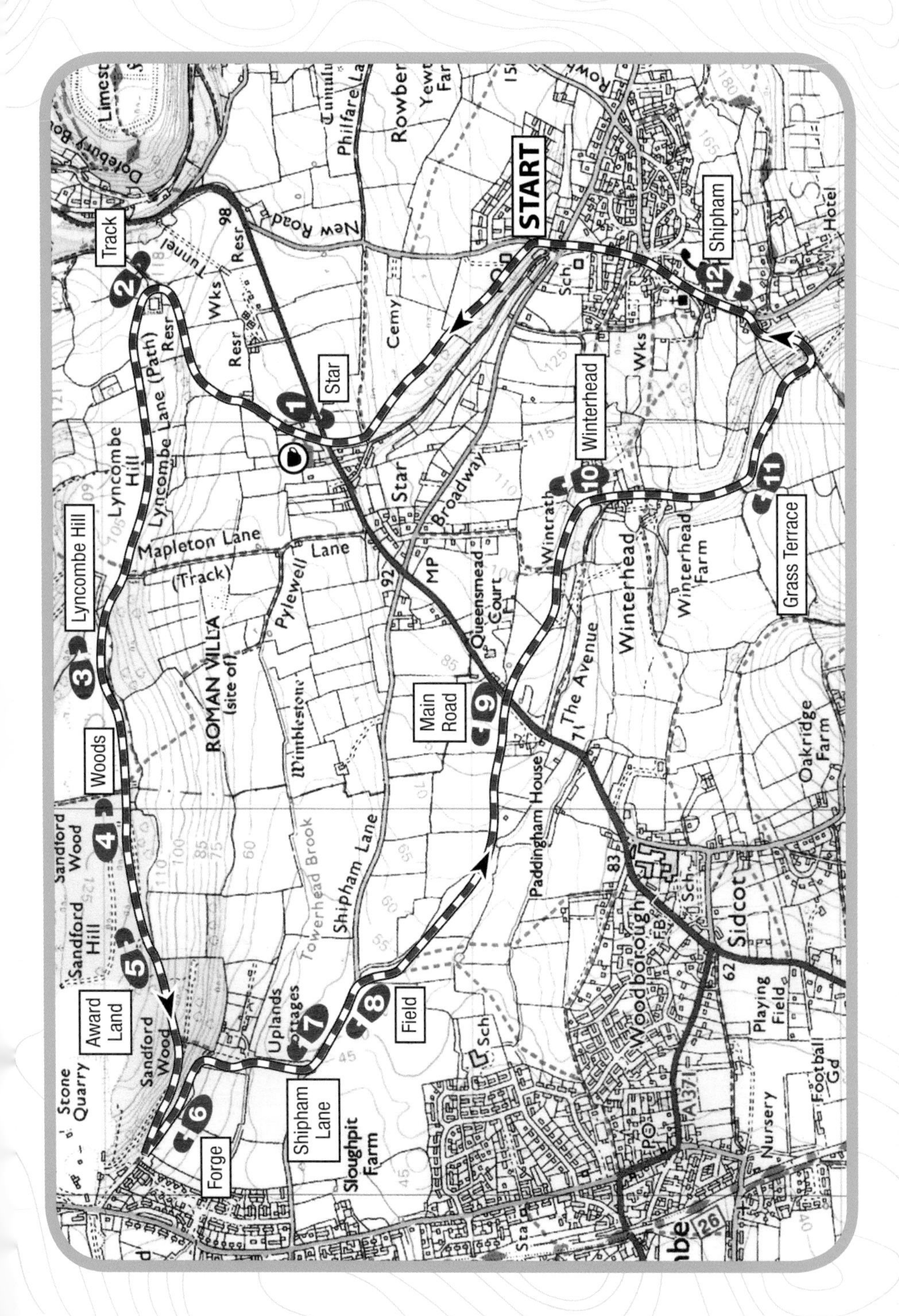
START
Track
Star
Lyncombe Hill
Woods
Award Land
Forge
Shipham Lane
Field
Main Road
Winterhead
Grass Terrace
Shipham
New Road
Tunnel
Wks
Resr
Cemy
Lyncombe Hill
Lyncombe Lane (Path)
Mapleton Lane
(Track)
Pylewell Lane
ROMAN VILLA
(site of)
Wimblestone
Towerhead Brook
Shipham Lane
Star
Broadway
Queensmead Court
Wintrath
The Avenue
Winterhead
Winterhead Farm
Paddingham House
Oakridge Farm
Sidcot
Woodborough
Playing Field
Football Gd
Nursery
Sandford Wood
Sandford Hill
Stone Quarry
Uplands Cottages
Sloughpit Farm
Philfare La
Dolebury
Hotel
A371

Shipham walk

A gentle circle from the old mining village of Shipham – one of very few villages on the central Mendip escarpment. Drop down through the hamlet of Star to pick up a track – once the main route to Bristol. Then head along Lyncombe Hill and follow field paths and tracks to reach Winterhead. Go through this old mining settlement and then up on to the hill above. It is easy walking with stiles that dogs should be able to negotiate. There are some ups and downs, and one steepish short hill. In Shipham is a welcoming small coffee shop and a pub. Not far into the walk you pass the Star pub.

MAP: OS Explorer 141 Cheddar Gorge & Mendip Hills West

GRID REF: 444 528

DISTANCE: 4.75 miles

TIME: About 2-3 hours walking

PARK: In Shipham, in the village hall car park. Park sensibly. If there will be more than 5 cars, please ring Kate Meadows, Booking Secretary (Telephone 01173 182 357) to check whether the hall will be busy that day. If so, you will need to park further into the village around the green and then pick up directions from 'SHIPHAM'. The village is on a road leading from the A38 and heading over the hill down to Shipham.

View from Lyncombe Hill

START: From the main car park head towards the entrance to the hall. Immediately, turn right on a footpath which goes down under trees (people who had to park in Shipham village will join here). The path comes out onto the open playing field. Continue on, cross a stile and carry on getting widespread views.

Descend through rather bumpy land – the remains of former lead mining. Go to the right of a closed reservoir and head down to the wall below. Turn left on the path alongside the wall. Cross right over a pipe stile and go through the field and onto the main road. Cross to The Star Inn.

STAR

Take the No Through Road to the right of the inn which is the old Bristol Road.

TRACK

At the top reach a bridleway track going left with a Bristol Water installation on the corner.

The very pure water from Mendip is of a quality very rarely seen in lowland Britain. This is due in the main to the filtration of the water through many layers of limestone.

Follow it along towards Lyncombe Hill. The path narrows. Ignore side paths. Gently climb and reach a gate ahead bringing us onto open land on the Hill.

LYNCOMBE HILL

Maintain direction all the way to a gate into Sandford Woods.

WOODS

Follow the track on through the woodland with a fence on the right around the former Sandford quarry.

Commercial quarrying for Burrington Oolite stone began on Sandford Hill in the mid c19th. Sandford stone was reputed to have been used in the construction of Avonmouth Docks opened in 1877 and in the expansion of Temple Meads Station, Bristol. However, even in 1885, the quarry appears to have had no direct connection to the branch railway line, only 300m away, which was an obvious drawback. The quarry ceased working in the mid 1990s. Parts of the site are now used by an activity centre and others converted to a nature reserve.

View to ➤
Crook Peak

➤ You will see that you are following the Butcombe Trail.

This is a 45 mile route devised by Sue Gearing and Les Davies several years ago that connects six Butcombe pubs.

Start to drop down.

AWARD LAND
Pass a sign on a tree for Winscombe and Sandford Award land.

This, and a nearby quarry, were awarded to the Parish in 1799 so they could dig out stone to rebuild local roads. It is now managed for public access and nature conservation by a group of local volunteers.

Reach a large metal gate on the right ahead and a sign for Mike's Path and take this.

It is named in memory of local man Mike Stone who did so much work in the area and was a dedicated naturalist. The path runs along the line of the old quarry railway.

Fork left down steps. At the foot, turn right for a quick detour of about 100 yards to old lime kilns which used limestone from Sandford Hill.

Then turn back to the forge.

Toll house

The old forge

FORGE

It was used to build steam crushers originally and later was reopened in World War II and worked by Italian prisoners of war and local men to make tools for the quarry.

Continue to a choice of paths ahead. Take the grassy one on the right known as the Uplands Path.

Pass the remains of a former toilet used by the prisoners of war.

Soon turn right down steps to join tarmac and keep straight on. Bend left by a large barn and then right up the drive.

SHIPHAM LANE

Turn left on Shipham Lane for a few minutes. Then, just before a track on the right, turn right over a stone slab stile into a field.

FIELD

Follow the left edge. Ahead is the edge of Winscombe. At the corner bear left along a narrow field. Cross onto a track and continue ahead to the A38.

MAIN ROAD

Cross to the drive opposite. Maintain direction.

WINTERHEAD

Reach a junction in the hamlet of Winterhead, formerly a lead mining settlement. Go straight ahead into the heart of this now peaceful place with a stream alongside. Continue on joining a rough track which leads into a field.

GRASS TERRACE

Go ahead towards the hill and then bear up onto a grassy terrace. Go into a field and follow the left edge. At the end come onto a crossing track and turn immediately left steeply downhill on steps to the stream and footbridge.

Climb up the other side, bend left and continue to rise. Cross a stile and carry on to the main road on the edge of Shipham.

SHIPHAM

Turn right a few yards and then cross to the grass bank opposite. Go left on the footpath which soon becomes a raised tarmac path alongside the road. Follow this down to join the pavement and continue on into the centre. Come to the Penscot if you want refreshment and opposite is Lenny's Coffee Shop up on the green by the Square.

Continue on, passing the primary school left and then the old Turnpike Cottage on the corner of Broadway. Cross back by the 30 mile limit sign to take the path by the village noticeboard to the village hall.

(If you parked in Shipham village, don't go into the car park but take the path ahead at the side which goes under trees and follow directions at the beginning).

Penscot Inn, Shipham	The Star Inn, Star	Lenny's Coffee Shop
01934 842659	**01934 844453**	**Closed Sat, Sun, Mon**

View from the ridge

Priddy
walk

IN LOVING MEMORY OF OUR DEAR
DAUGHTER CATHERINE GIBBONS
TAKEN FROM US ON THE 6TH DAY
OF OCTOBER 1988 AGED 19 YEARS

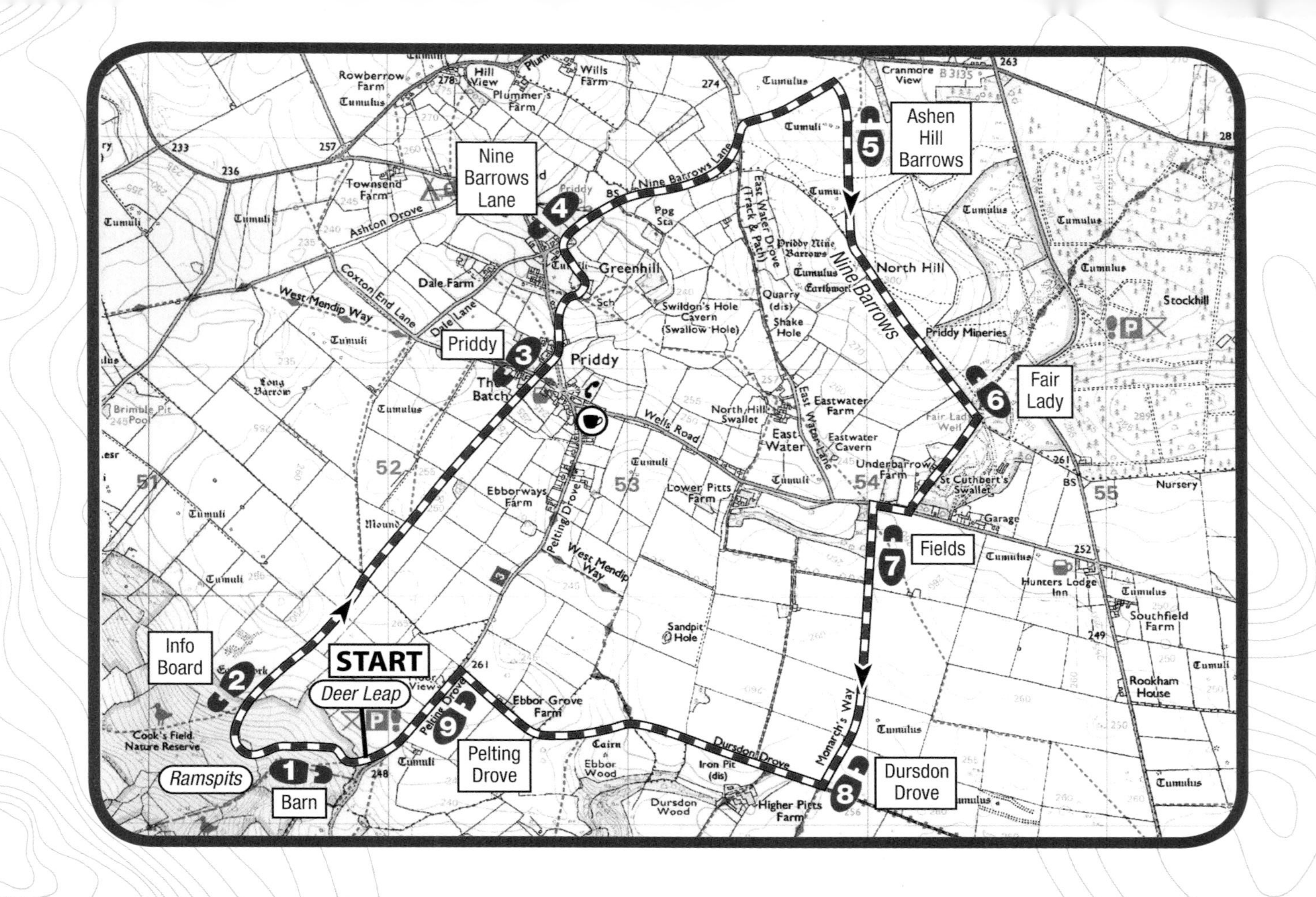
START
Deer Leap
Barn
Ramspits
Info Board
Priddy
Nine Barrows Lane
Ashen Hill Barrows
Fair Lady
Fields
Dursdon Drove
Pelting Drove
Nine Barrows
Monarch's Way
West Mendip Way
Cook's Field Nature Reserve
Stockhill
Priddy Mineries
North Hill
Greenhill
Hunters Lodge Inn

Priddy walk

A level and very diverse circle reaching into the heart of Mendip mainly up on the flat escarpment with old stone walls, the song of the skylark and stupendous south facing views. It takes in Priddy village with the famous hurdle stack, and the ancient round barrows up on North Hill. It also explores ancient field systems and communities, mining and caving. There are quite a few stiles, but no steep hills. Go well wrapped up as it can be windy and exposed.

MAP: OS Explorer 141 Cheddar Gorge & Mendip Hills West

GRID REF: 518 492

DISTANCE: 6.8 miles

TIME: About 4 hours walking

PARK: Just to the south of Priddy village, the highest on Mendip. From the green take the road right just past the phone box and go past the Queen Victoria pub a popular Butcombe pub. After about 1.25 miles on the road - known as Pelting Drove - arrive at a parking area, viewpoint and picnic site on the right on the edge of the escarpment – Deer Leap.

Priddy Church

START: Go through the wooden kissing gate in the side of the car park into a field known as Ramspits.

The field gets its name from the Norman, Lord William de Ramspute. It contains two deserted medieval farm settlements, ancient trackways and field systems.

Follow the well worn grass path ahead and when you see a low stone barn down on the left ahead, make your way to it across the rough grass and past many emmet tumps (anthills).

BARN

Reach the barn, originally a thatched two storey bank barn, built into the bank, probably used for oxen. In front of it is the remains of the former drinking pond.

The barn is the most visible remains of the medieval settlement of Ramspits and was restored by Somerset County Council for use by groups. This is a post medieval building that would have originally had a double pitched thatched roof. The lower floor was for animals, whilst the upper storey would have stored fodder. Note the poem on the wall in memory of a former manager with the Council.

From the barn, head straight down the bank past the old elm tree towards the edge of the hill for about 50 yards and soon reach a crossing old medieval trackway.

Turn right on the track and it leads across to a wall and ladder stile.

Once over come into an area of grassy lynchets below you.

Looking over the valley

These were the medieval strip field systems that stayed in use up until the Enclosures Acts of the late 1700s. The terracing has occurred because of the constant one way ploughing that took place over hundreds of years. We get a measurement of distance from these, the 'furlong', is 200m or 220 yards. This was the distance many of the lynchets were ploughed - the "furrow long".

Turn up a path to the right and follow the line of the wall to a kissing gate above.

Take time to stop and stare here at the amazing view over the Somerset Levels once flooded and hills like Glastonbury Tor and Nyland Hill were islands

Go through the kissing gate, follow the right wall up to the top corner with an information board.

2 INFORMATION BOARD

Cross the stile leaving the open access land. Go straight up – not along the wall. Soon meet a wall corner. Continue on up and reach an old stone slab stile with an interesting home-made metal gate in front to keep the cattle from 'storming'the stile.

Now simply keep straight on for nearly a mile across several fields and stiles on the high open farmland on the escarpment. Ignore any side paths.

On the way, just before woodland on the right, is a large depression - one of many swallet holes on Mendip.

PRIDDY

The last stile leads onto a lane. Go down to reach Priddy about 800ft above sea level.

The name which has a Welsh influence means 'of the earth', one of the very few Celtic names to survive on Mendip.

Come to Priddy green with the famous hurdle stack. ➤

Priddy hurdle stack

This is purely symbolic these days, but was originally the stack of sheep hurdles that were used to pen the sheep on Fair day. It's believed to have come to Priddy around 1348 from the City of Wells.

For the very welcoming Butcombe pub, the Queen Victoria, take a five minute detour right across the green to the phone box and then right a short way down the road (which you probably drove along).

To continue, go along the bottom edge of the green past Manor Farm - a caving mecca and the entrance to Swildons Hole Cavern.

Turn left on the lane and reach the village noticeboard. Behind it is the site of the former water supply for Priddy - the village wasn't connected to the mains until the mid 1950s.

Follow the raised pavement and then fork up right. At the top turn right towards the village hall, the primary school and church. Turn left on the path just before the school and reach the stone church with its natural churchyard – a haven for wild flowers.

The church tower is a nesting site for jackdaws.

Go past the church (right) and out the other side through a gate. Then on along to another gate and onto Nine Barrows Lane.

4 NINE BARROWS LANE
Turn right. Reach Priddy Pool.

This is one of very few ponds on Mendip because the limestone soil doesn't collect water but allows it to seep through – hence the caving systems below.

Follow the lane for nearly half a mile to reach a gate on the right into an open area on the edge of North Hill. We will reach the Ashen Hill barrows – you can just see one ahead – but need to follow the official footpath which bears left heading towards the line of firs in the distance.

5 ASHEN HILL BARROWS
Pass to the right of a single barrow and continue on. You now have the line of Ashen Hill barrows right.

Ashen Hill barrows

One of the very few ponds on Mendip

Along with the Priddy Nine Barrows which we reach soon, these are ancient burial mounds. Reach a telegraph pole and turn up right towards the line of barrows. Go through between the third and fourth barrow from the left. Then head on, cross a very visible stile and continue towards the Nine Barrows which are divided into seven barrows and a pair slightly separated. Pass them.

Continue to follow the wall, passing Bristol Water reservoir.

Mendip is a huge 'limestone sponge' that releases about 72 million gallons of water, (324million litres) from Mendip every day! Bristol Water was set up in the mid 1800s to supply Bristol with clean water from Mendip.

In the corner cross a stile into a rough area, part of the land of the old Priddy Mineries.

This is the site of the last lead smelting works on Mendip. It was finally closed in 1910 because the water contamination it was causing in Wookey Hole affected the paper mill that needed a ready supply of very clean water. The closure was made easier because the paper company owned the lead works as well.

Follow the path downhill and bend round to reach a clear crossing path below. Turn right and soon see ahead left the pond which is fed by Fairlady Well.

6 FAIRLADY

Just before the pond, at the footpath marker, turn right. Here is the spring/well.
We have now joined the Monarch's Way which follows a leat leading from the well.

The Way is a 615-mile footpath from Worcester to Brighton that follows the escape route of King Charles II in 1651 after his defeat in the Battle of Worcester.

Over left see undulating spoil heaps - the remains of St Cuthbert's Minery, the largest lead smelting works on Mendip.

Underneath us is another cave system, St Cuthbert's Swallet.

The path bends right and reaches the end of a drive.

Cross and go over the pipe stile opposite and through grounds of the Belfry caving club. Go past their front door and out to the road.

Turn right for a few minutes. Just past the last cottage on the right, cross the stile left on the marked footpath.

FIELDS

Go straight ahead with the fence and trees right and continue through several fields all in the same direction for 0.75 miles and come onto the crossing Dursdon Drove. En route ignore the West Mendip Way.

DURSDON DROVE

Dursdon Drove is one of the many ancient roadways – super-highways of the Middle Ages - used to move livestock around the hill.

Turn right and after just over a mile reach another drove, now a road.

PELTING DROVE

Go left for 0.3 miles towards the escarpment edge. At a footpath marker bear off right and this small path leads you back to the parking area.

The Queen Victoria
01749 676385

Les Davies on the ladder stile

East Harptree
walk

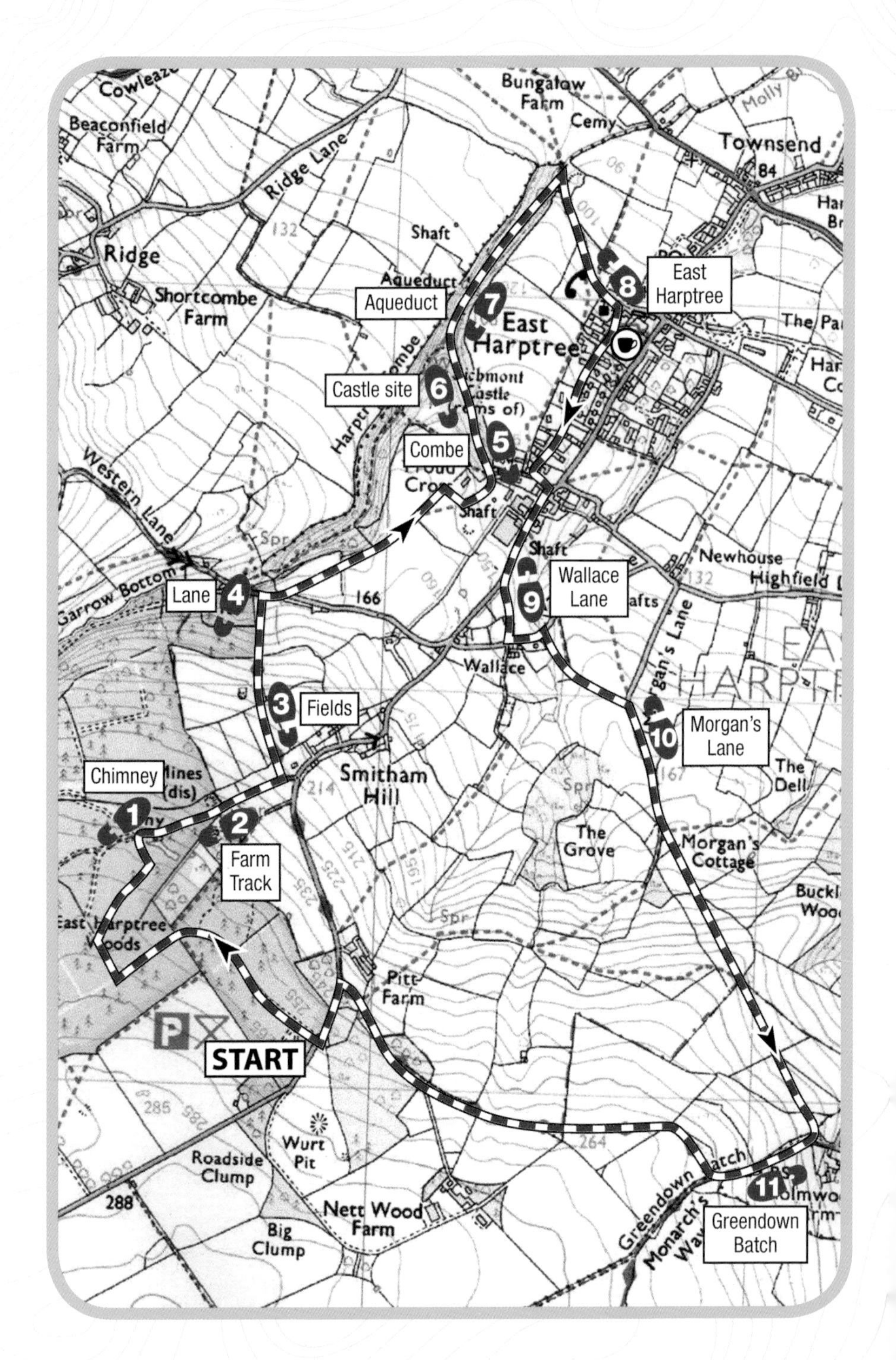
START
Chimney
Farm Track
Fields
Lane
Combe
Castle site
Aqueduct
East Harptree
Wallace Lane
Morgan's Lane
Greendown Batch
East Harptree
Smitham Hill
Ridge
Shortcombe Farm
Beaconfield Farm
Ridge Lane
Western Lane
Garrow Bottom
Townsend
Bungalow Farm
Pitt Farm
Nett Wood Farm
Roadside Clump
Big Clump
Wurt Pit
The Grove
Morgan's Cottage
Newhouse
Monarch's Way
The Dell

East Harptree walk

This beautiful circle in the centre of the Mendip Hills Area of Outstanding Natural Beauty near East Harptree weaves together an important part of Mendip's mining history, Mendip's valuable water supply and the site of a c12th ruined castle. It starts at East Harptree woods, visits the last lead smelting chimney on Mendip and then descends following the flow of water as it starts its amazing journey by gravity feed to Bristol. In Harptree Combe is the site of a castle with a dramatic history. After going through East Harptree village, where there is a pub, we climb back up steadily getting great views over Chew Valley Lake and beyond. There are very few stiles so it is a very good dog walk too.

MAP: OS Explorer 141 Cheddar Gorge & Mendip Hills West

GRID REF: 558 541

DISTANCE: 5.1 miles

TIME: About 3 hours walking

PARK: In the free car park at East Harptree Woods in the care of the Forestry Commission. This is up above East Harptree village, to the south, and can be reached from the village or from the road opposite the Castle of Comfort Inn up on the B3134 cross Mendip road. The turn is signed to East Harptree and the car park entrance is through a barrier in woodland on the left before you drop downhill.
(Do not leave valuables in your car).

View to Chew Valley Lake

START: From the pretty parking and picnic area turn left on the broad track through the woods, part of a circular walking route round Mendip, the Mendip Ring. Continue all the way until you reach a right turn clearly marked to Smitham Chimney. Follow this through Frances Plantation, in memory of Frances, Countess of Waldegrave. (The Waldegrave family seat is at Chewton Mendip). Follow this round to a pond with Smitham Chimney facing you.

CHIMNEY

Here stands the last lead smelting chimney on Mendip. It is all that remains of the industrial-scale lead processing that took place on this site. The condensor flues have long ago fallen into ruin and the smelter taken down. This chimney is built in the Cornish style, with a flared stone base rising to brick built and iron banded upper courses. This structure was saved and re-building made possible with help from the Mendip Society. A board tells you more, and an artist's impression gives a feeling of the industrialisation of this area. (Can you spot the 'Michael Jackson' like figure pushing the cart!).

Smitham Chimney

In 1887 the Harptree Hoard was discovered near the chimney by a local labourer. This was in a Roman pewter pot with ingots of silver and proved of interest to the British Museum which took some of the hoard.

But other coins went to East Harptree church and unfortunately were stolen in the early 1970s.

Follow the path round to an information plinth and then turn right passing close to the chimney. Bend left and start to descend. On your left, but now invisible under vegetation, were the old flues leading from a furnace.

This is the area of the condensor flues, where hot lead laden gas from the smelter travelled up and down a series of stone tunnels before entering the base of the chimney. The gases cooled in the tunnels and condensed, leaving lead deposits upon the floor and stonework of the tunnel. This was scraped out by miners, causing them lead and arsenic poisoning. The huge pile of sticks in the bottom of the chimney are the remains of frustrated attempts by jackdaws nest building in the chimney.

2 FARM TRACK

Keep straight on, go through a gate and yard and on down the farm track. After another gate, turn left and come into a field (still on the Mendip Ring).

3 FIELDS

Cross the field to a kissing gate on the far side and head to the next bottom right corner. Go through two kissing gates on the edge of an area of woodland, full of ransoms or wild garlic in Spring. Then follow the left field edge down and out onto a lane.

4 LANE

On the left is a valley called 'Garrow Bottom', the source of an important spring that feeds the water supply into Bristol.

Turn right. Shortly, go through a gate following the footpath marker into a field. Go straight down, through a gate on the far side, and continue on as before, heading towards the edge of the hill. After going through a large field gate, follow a fenced path down the left side and then along the bottom of the field by a house and round to the left. Ahead in the field see a square stone plinth which is one of several air vents above Bristol Water's line of works.

wild garlic

When you consider that this pipe which is part of the 'line of works' was built in the mid 1800s it is an amazing feat of engineering. By gravity alone it still takes water from Mendip each day to the filtration beds at Barrow, south of Bristol. Here at Proud Cross Farm it runs about 100 feet below the surface.

In the next corner go out left down through a large gate to an area known as Proud Cross.

COMBE

Turn left through a gate into woodland and Harptree Combe and on down the trackway. Pass under another vent and have a look down into it to see the amazing depth of this Victorian structure.

CASTLE SITE

Shortly reach a small copse of beech trees and a track going up left. Here you can make a short detour up to the old castle site. Follow this up to the top. Very little remains of the old structure – only some stone from the original curtain wall - but it is an atmospheric place.

The castle, set amid such beauty, must have seen much cruelty and drama. The original owner was the notorious Azeline de Percheval, so vicious he was known as the Wolf, and his equally cruel son, known as the Wolf Cub. Later it was owned by the Gourney family and was probably used in the Norman conquest of Somersetshire and was almost impregnable. In 1138 it was held for the Empress Matilda by Sir William de Harptree against Stephen, fresh from the siege of Bristol. He managed to capture it through a ruse which lured the defenders out and the attackers went round the back. The king, however, did not destroy the castle. It was pulled down in Henry VIII's reign.

Calamine mining went on spasmodically round the site of the old castle until the mid c19th.

Down right against the rocky side of the stream is the hardly visible remains of a once much visited wishing well.

Dramatic Victorian aqueduct

Retrace your steps down to the lower track and turn left, passing another air shaft. Shortly, it is worth another short detour up steps left to see the man-made conduit which funnels the water from the stream into the large piped aqueduct you pass under soon.

Return to the track below and continue on, soon following a stone slab path by the stream with a huge stone supporting bank on the right and reach the dramatic Victorian aqueduct.

7 AQUEDUCT

Great civil engineering and fine stonework!

Go under and continue to the end of the combe, crossing the first stile of the walk. Turn right, climbing gently, going between hedges and then across to East Harptree church.

8 EAST HARPTREE

Cross a raised stone stile with an interesting boot hole at the bottom.

This light and airy church has an interesting c16th monument in the porch to Sir John Newton with his twenty children dutifully kneeling in a row.

Go along the path to the village and the Waldegrave Arms opposite.

Turn right on the lane through the village. Bend left and at a junction turn right on the lane which soon leaves the village climbing gently.

9 WALLACE LANE

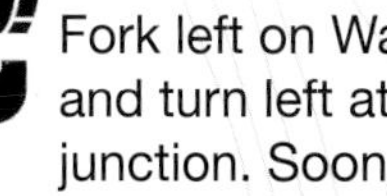

Fork left on Wallace Lane and turn left at the next junction. Soon, on the corner, go right on the marked footpath through a Bristol Gate into a field.

These useful gates were born from an idea by the Bristol Footpath Wardens in the old County of Avon days. They allow for field security by a locked main gate but free pedestrian access through the smaller gate.

Gently climb up through the field with the stream down right. Go through a gate and turn left along the hedge. This leads along to Morgan's Lane.

MORGAN'S LANE

Follow this No Through Lane up to Morgan's Cottage and take the track to the left continuing up. At the end, a gate leads into a field. Head uphill passing to the right of an oak and bushes above. The bottom part of the field is quite wet and marshy from a spring rising further up. Keep on in the middle of the field and go through a gate on the far side. Cross the field to the right of a power pole. Cross a stile and maintain direction. Look for a stile half way along the right hedge. Once over, head across to a stile into woodland. Follow a short sunken track and immediately turn right up a stony track, Greendown Batch.

Line of works air vent

GREENDOWN BATCH

After several minutes, go right through a marked Bristol Gate, back on the Mendip Ring and Monarch's Way. Go ahead through two fields, with great views down right, and then start to bear up left to the edge where you join a track and continue on.

On the field boundary you will notice a stone bank topped by a hedgerow. This is a Devon bank, or a Cornish hedge, (dependant on which side of the Tamar river you stand) an unusual sight on Mendip. These were built by the Knight family who had come here from Devon.

Go through a gate onto a hard track and continue to the lane.

Turn up left and soon reach the car park in East Harptree Woods.

The Waldegrave Arms
01761 221429

Closed Monday lunchtime, but may open for a group. Call to check current situation.

Bishop Sutton
walk

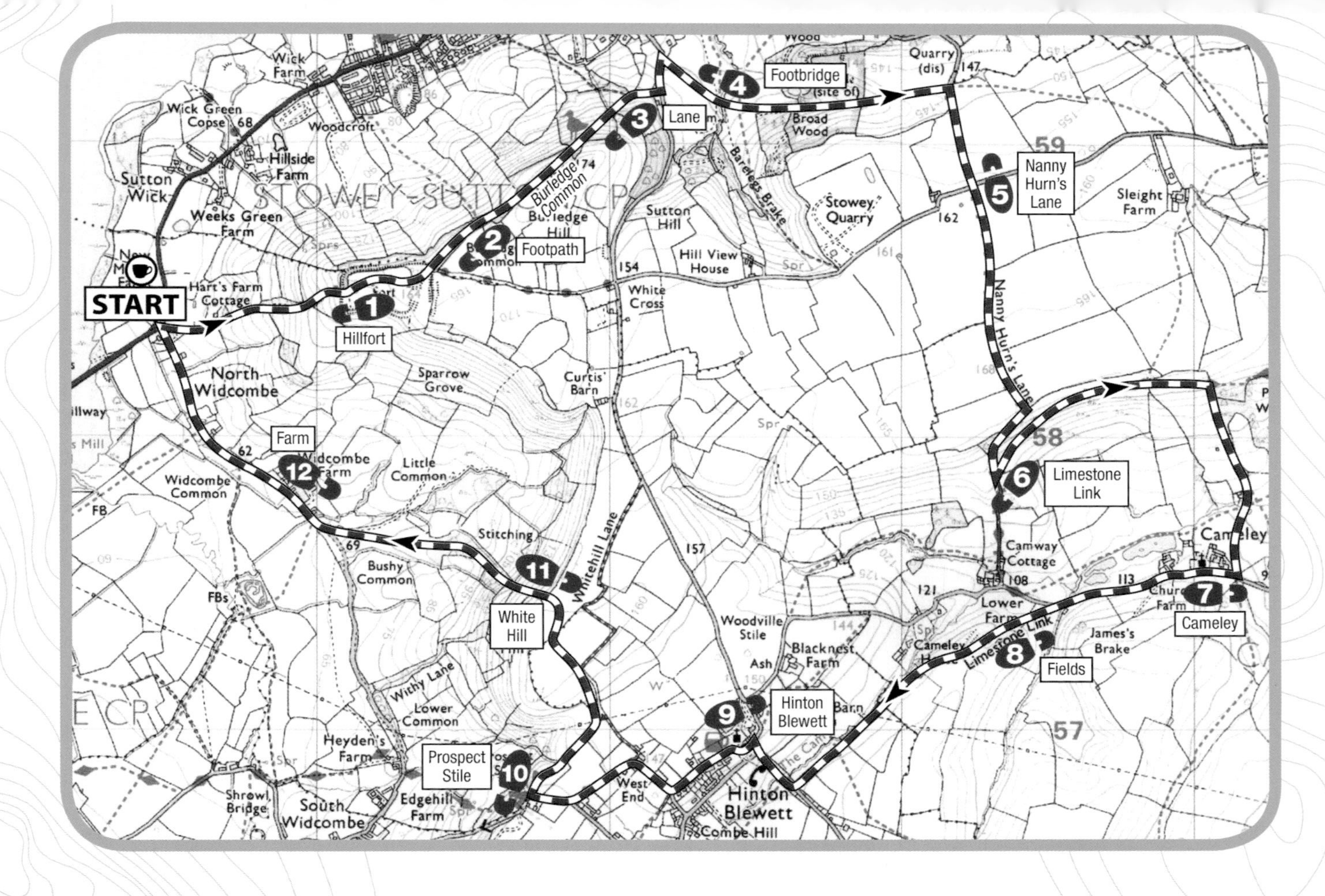
START
Hillfort
Footpath
Lane
Footbridge
Nanny Hurn's Lane
Limestone Link
Cameley
Fields
Hinton Blewett
Prospect Stile
White Hill
Farm

Bishop Sutton walk

Some of the most breathtaking views of the Chew Valley are your reward for climbing 15 minutes onto Burledge Hill at the beginning of this circle. Start fairly early from New Manor Farm near Bishop Sutton so you have time, not only to enjoy different views across to Mendip, but also to visit the memorable little church at Cameley. This should then get you to Hinton Blewett to enjoy the pub in the heart of the village. After another great viewpoint, drop down the hill and back across Burledge Common to the start. Manor Farm has an outstanding cafe as well as a farm shop and a shop selling country antiques.

MAP: OS Explorer 141 Cheddar Gorge & Mendip Hills West

GRID REF: 573 584 (also goes into Explorer 142)

DISTANCE: 7.5 miles

TIME: About 3.5 hours walking

PARK: At New Manor Farm on the A368 near West Harptree and just south of Bishop Sutton, close by Herriots Bridge on the east of Chew Valley lake.

Looking down on Cameley

START: Go out the farm drive and right on the fenced path alongside the road. Shortly, at the first junction, cross to go up the byway. After a barrier this soon becomes a rough track which climbs Burledge Hill.

HILLFORT

After about 15 minutes come up to the hillfort and the open grassy top in front of you with evidence of earthworks around, but no information board.

This hillfort is one of many in this area that would have controlled the high ground and approaches. They were built not because of a threat, but more in case of a threat. Here, safe behind the earthworks and wooden walls, the inhabitants could have withstood attack. Such places were also important centres for trade during the Iron Age. Evidence of iron working has been found here.

The first of the impressive views are here across Chew Valley Lake.

This is the second 'man made' lake that was created by flooding the Chew Valley area. It was opened in the 1950s by the Queen.

Continue on the track, with more of the hillfort on your left and right.

FOOTPATH

Reach a more open area at a junction of tracks and go left on a public footpath, staying close to a hedge right, on the other side of which is Burledge Common. Continue along the hedge, ignoring side paths, passing between two steel posts. Ignore a side footpath with handrail. Go through a kissing gate and here is the most spectacular panorama of all, looking across to Wales as well as over the lake to Knowle Hill and beyond. Down below is the village of Bishop Sutton.

Bishop Sutton grew up around coal mining from the mid 1800s to the late 1920s, when the Somerset coal seams were being exploited throughout this area.

Cross a field, keeping straight on, staying high and at a marker post, descend following the path all the way down, using steps, going through gates and reaching a lane by a house.

LANE

Go down left and shortly turn right through a Bristol Gate on a public footpath. Follow the fence round, through a kissing gate and head across a field following the footpath arrow.

FOOTBRIDGE

Cross a footbridge over a stream. Go straight on, slightly left; heading towards the 'v' of a valley. Go through another gate and on through the valley ahead. Up on the other side of the wooded hill left is the site of a former castle.

This was Stowey Castle, an Iron Age hill fort that may have been re-used during the Middle Ages. Note the animal feeding terraces on the grassy slopes of the valley, particularly on the left. These are created by grazing animals standing sideways along the slope to feed. As they move along they create these mini terraces over a period of time.

Maintain direction all the way up to the top, going through another gate.

Go over a stile by a gate onto a lane. Turn right (there may be some traffic along here) and after 4-5 minutes reach a bend and junction.

NANNY HURN'S LANE

Go straight ahead on another old byway, known as Nanny Hurn's Lane. (After rain, expect large puddles). There are views across right to the Mendip ridge. Follow the track along and then bend right downhill where you should see bluebells on the bank in Spring. On the way down, look left to a stile into a field and the Limestone Link marker.

Hand-operated slurry pump

LIMESTONE LINK

The Limestone Link is a 36 mile footpath that links the limestone of Cotswold with that of the Mendip Hills. It starts at Cold Ashton, South Gloucestershire and ends at Shipham in Somerset.

This Link footpath takes you up across the side of the hill full of 'emmet tumps' (anthills) going back on yourself for a while. Pass through a kissing gate and a metal gate close together and then keep on, staying above trees and scrub. Start to get views down right over Cameley hamlet, church and fishing lakes. At a marker post near the end of the field, turn right on the Limestone Link and immediately left through two kissing gates which may be obscured by vegetation. Go ahead across the field and at the wood on the far side, turn down right descending, still in the field. Go through a Bristol Gate and follow the short footpath along the right edge. In the corner, go through a gate and then over a footbridge over the Cam Brook.

It's worth going down right to look at the old bridge at the side and particularly at the structure of the arch with the key stone in the centre. This key stone was discovered by the Romans and allowed them to build arches. The larger key stone at the centre of the arch distributes the weight sideways and down thus locking together structures such as this bridge.

Head straight on with the church ahead and right. Follow the footpath through a gate and yard and then go left into the field at the side, and turn right to come out onto the drive. Follow this to the road in Cameley.

CAMELEY

Turn right and soon reach a real gem of an ancient English country church, St James, nestling between ancient yews and tombstones.

It is now redundant and cared for by the Churches Conservation Trust.

It was called 'Rip Van Winkle's church' by Sir John Betjeman because there has been little change there since the early part of the c19th. The church itself dates back to the c13th.

The c15th tower is built of red Mendip stone which contrasts with the local blue lias limestone of the rest of the church. Inside there are fine box pews, and a gallery. It is well worth looking in the guide book to find out more about the church's fascinating history.

Continue on the lane, passing Cameley Lodge and fishing lakes (there may be a sign offering coffee and tea). At the right bend leave the lane and go left through a kissing gate rejoining the Limestone Link.

8 FIELDS

Head diagonally right up the field, through into another and turn uphill left. At the top continue straight on through fields coming close to Cam Brook.

Eventually come out on to a lane opposite Hinton Blewett village hall, formerly the village school.

Turn right uphill into Hinton Blewett.

9 HINTON BLEWETT

The original settlement of 'Hantone', meaning 'high enclosure or town' in Old English, was later remodelled as a medieval planned village like others in the area.

Go up across the green *(known as the Barbary)* to the welcoming pub, the Ring O' Bells. Turn left in front of the pub and follow the lane round to the right. Continue to a bend by West End Farm and follow it round left. At a T-junction go right.

St James Church

PROSPECT STILE

Before long come to another junction with Prospect Stile ahead, another great viewpoint with seats – looking across to Chew and Blagdon lakes and Mendip. Turn right on the track. Further along by a small ford go up on the dryer path on the left. At a junction of tracks, go left over a stile into a field. Head up parallel with the right edge, passing close to a power pole. Go through a kissing gate in the corner. Now cross the field, bearing slightly right to an indent along the far side. Here is another kissing gate, stile and permissive access.

WHITE HILL

Take the public footpath straight ahead. Watch your footing as it descends steeply down the hillside following the edge. Down below on the left is a kissing gate – where it may be a little muddy and wet. Go through and down under trees in an area known as the Stitching.

Leave the wood through a gate and take the permissive path down the right side of the field and through a Bristol Gate in the corner. Once through, head straight down the field to a Bristol Gate near the bottom left corner and onto a lane.

FARM

Turn right passing North Widcombe Farm, owned by the Duchy of Cornwall. Continue on past Widcombe Common and come out onto the A368. Cross with care and turn right back to New Manor Farm.

New Manor Farm teashop
01761 220172

Ring O'Bells
01761 452239

Looking over the lake and Denny Island

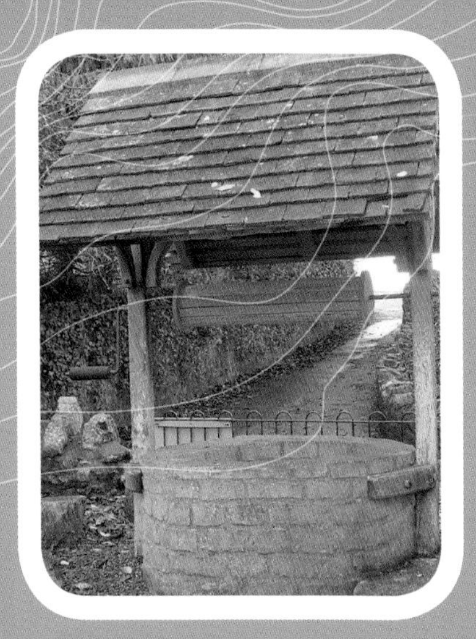

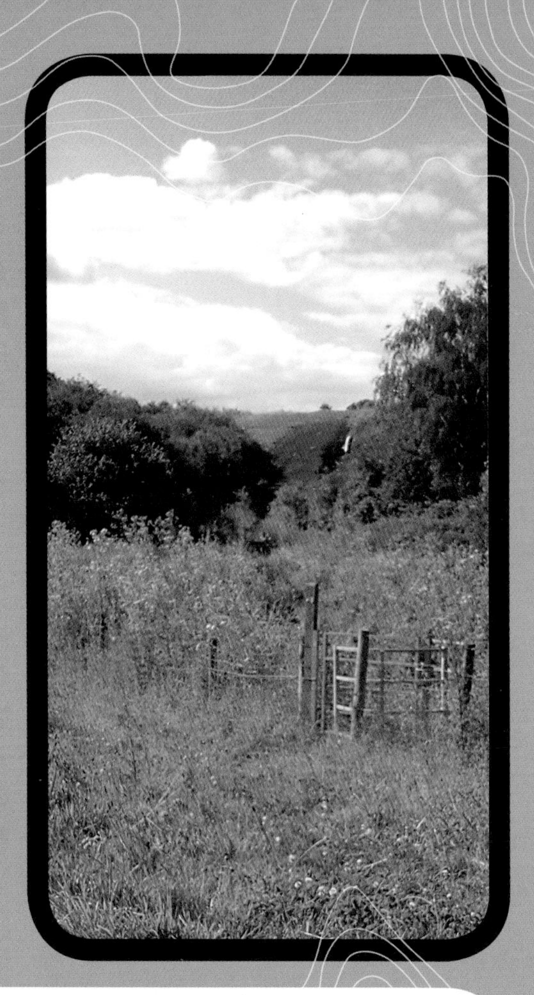

Radstock
walk

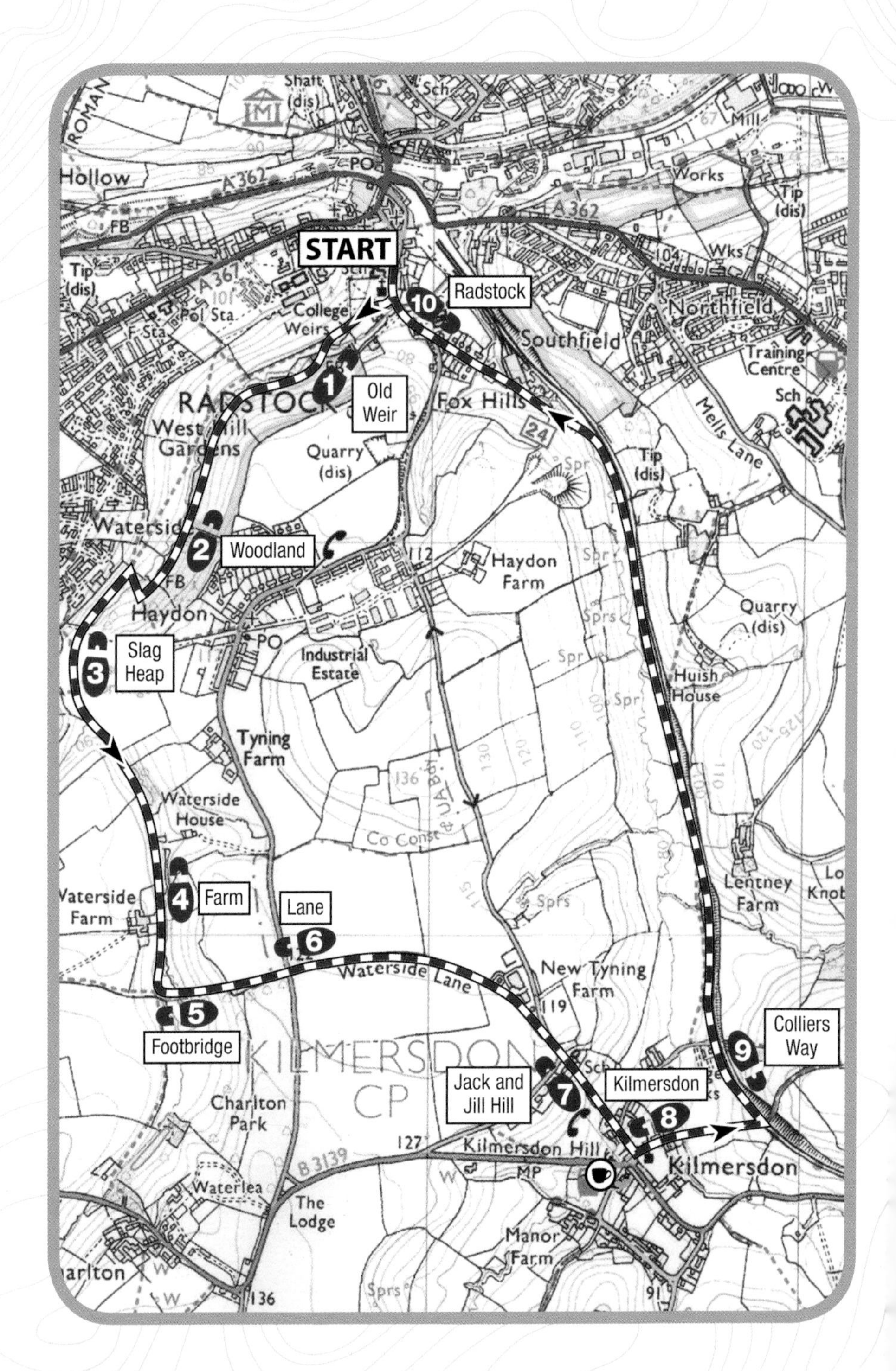

START
Radstock
Old Weir
Woodland
Slag Heap
Farm
Lane
Footbridge
Jack and Jill Hill
Kilmersdon
Colliers Way
1
2
3
4
5
6
7
8
9
10

Radstock walk

Step out in the footsteps of coal miners in East Somerset along the Wellow Brook and into the land of nursery rhymes from Radstock. It is a landscape transformed into a green and pleasant place after coal mining ceased in the late 1960s. Finish the walk along a disused railway, now the Colliers Way, a walk and cycleway. Drop down the famous Jack and Jill hill to Kilmersdon with a pub. At the start is a very friendly cafe. There are a couple of slopes but otherwise it's flat and easy with only two stiles. A visit to Radstock Museum would be good to round it off.

MAP: OS Explorer 142 Shepton Mallet & Mendip Hills East

GRID REF: 688 546

DISTANCE: 4.25 miles

TIME: About 2.5 hours walking

PARK: In the centre of Radstock. On the A37 take the road opposite the Co-op signed to Haydon off the roundabout. Bear right into Church Street and park up on the right in the free car park (get a free ticket).

View from Jack and Jill hill

START: *Radstock has been settled since the Iron Age. Its importance grew with the construction of the Fosse Way, the Roman road that ran along what is now part of the A367 in Radstock.*

With industrialisation, Radstock became a transport centre, with the Great Western Railway, the Somerset and Dorset Railway, and the terminus of the southern branch of the Somerset Coal Canal, (turned into a tramway in 1815).

Many mines opened during the c19th - several owned by the Waldegrave family, the Lords of the Manor. (Admiral Lord Radstock, brother of George, fourth Earl Waldegrave, took the town's name as his title when created a Baron.)

Turn right into Church Street and pass St Nicholas church. Then go right to the community centre where volunteers run a friendly cafe (open weekdays 11am-3pm). Go down the side of the centre with churchyard right, through a kissing gate and on along the track. Very shortly look left for a short path and kissing gate (somewhat hidden).

lychgate

OLD WEIR

This takes you over a bridge by an interesting old weir on the Wellow Brook. Turn right alongside the brook. Maintain direction through grass that may be long in this Open Access Area. Continue all the way to woodland.

WOODLAND

Enter through a kissing gate and stay on the main path keeping the stream in sight on your right until you rise to leave the wood. Approach an area of disused slag. Rise gently to a junction of paths. Go down right and into woodland to join a raised path. Climb towards houses and before the top, turn left on a clear path. Soon cross a wooden footbridge and carry on under trees. Out in the open, climb a little.

SLAG HEAP

At a junction of paths, go up left onto the slag heap. After a few yards turn right again. Below you can see a footpath and kissing gate – your goal. If you wish, drop fairly steeply off the slag heap here. For a more

Colliers Way railway

gentle drop, go right on a small path downhill and immediately left on a smaller path into woodland going round the foot of the slope. There's a kissing gate and footbridge and then bear up left to a Bristol Gate.

Work is being done to deal with this muddy section of about 50 yards. After the second Bristol Gate keep straight on, going through gates.

FARM

Pass Waterside Farm up right. Keep on as before making sure you follow the footpath arrow. Pass a pond left. At another wooden gate, reach a crossing of tracks with a stile ahead. Turn left on the flat and then cross the stream on a small stone footbridge to the left of the ford.

FOOTBRIDGE

Go ahead up the hill with the park-like setting of Charlton Park on your right. Look over right to see the main house.

Go ahead up hill. Look back for a view across country to Radstock. At the top cross the stile and go down the field edge. At the end cross onto the road.

LANE

Cross with care and follow the quiet lane ahead. Pass a farm and at the T-junction, go right to Kilmersdon school where the Jack and Jill adventure begins. At the bend go ahead down the No Through path past the school.

JACK AND JILL HILL

This is the top of Jack and Jill Hill of nursery rhyme fame.

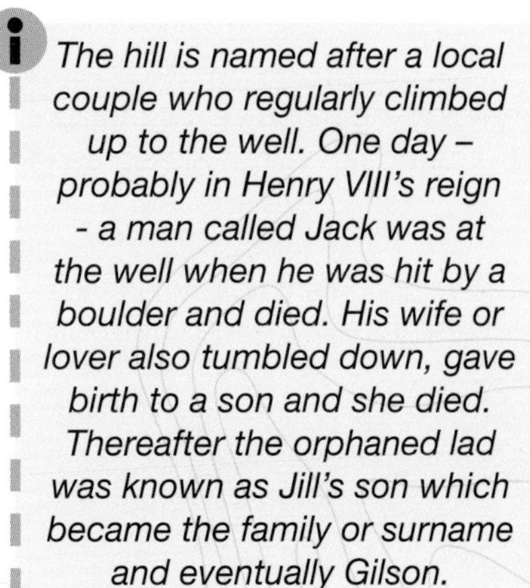

The hill is named after a local couple who regularly climbed up to the well. One day – probably in Henry VIII's reign - a man called Jack was at the well when he was hit by a boulder and died. His wife or lover also tumbled down, gave birth to a son and she died. Thereafter the orphaned lad was known as Jill's son which became the family or surname and eventually Gilson.

Reach the well by the school. >

The Jack and Jill Millennium project discovered a Medieval well shaft and built this well head above. Notice the children's slate drawings on the walls from the rhyme.

Go on downhill on the tarmac passing stone verses.

On your right is the original old hollow-way - possibly the route taken by Jack and Jill.

KILMERSDON

At the foot, turn right in Kilmersdon village. Shortly at the junction go right. Reach the church which is well worth a visit. It has a handsome stone lychgate and impressive yew trees in the churchyard.

For The Jolliffe Arms go on along the lane a couple more minutes to the main road.

For our circle turn left in Church Street. At the end follow the footpath into a field and straight up the edge. Take a path left which drops down to the old railway, the Colliers Way. Turn left.

COLLIERS WAY

This is part of the National Cycle network using the route of the old railway. As part of the development of the Wilts, Somerset and Weymouth railway, an 8-mile line from Radstock to Frome was built to carry coal. In the 1870s this was converted to standard gauge and connected to other rail lines. The last passenger train service in Radstock closed in 1966, and the last coal mines in 1973.

There are seats along the way and apple trees, harking back to the days when train passengers threw apple cores out - many of which took root. Artists worked with local schools to develop a 'linear orchard' by the old track celebrating the importance of apples in Somerset.

Reach coloured stripes on the ground - an intriguing 70 yard project developed by Katy Hallett. The stripes represent the code for the gene BRCA2 that plays an important role in our bodies, producing a protein that helps repair human DNA.

RADSTOCK

After just over 1.25 miles reach new housing ahead on the edge of Radstock and go left. This leads through a residential road to Church Street. Turn right back to the start.

The Jolliffe Arms, Kilmersdon
01761 436699

Buckland Dinham
walk

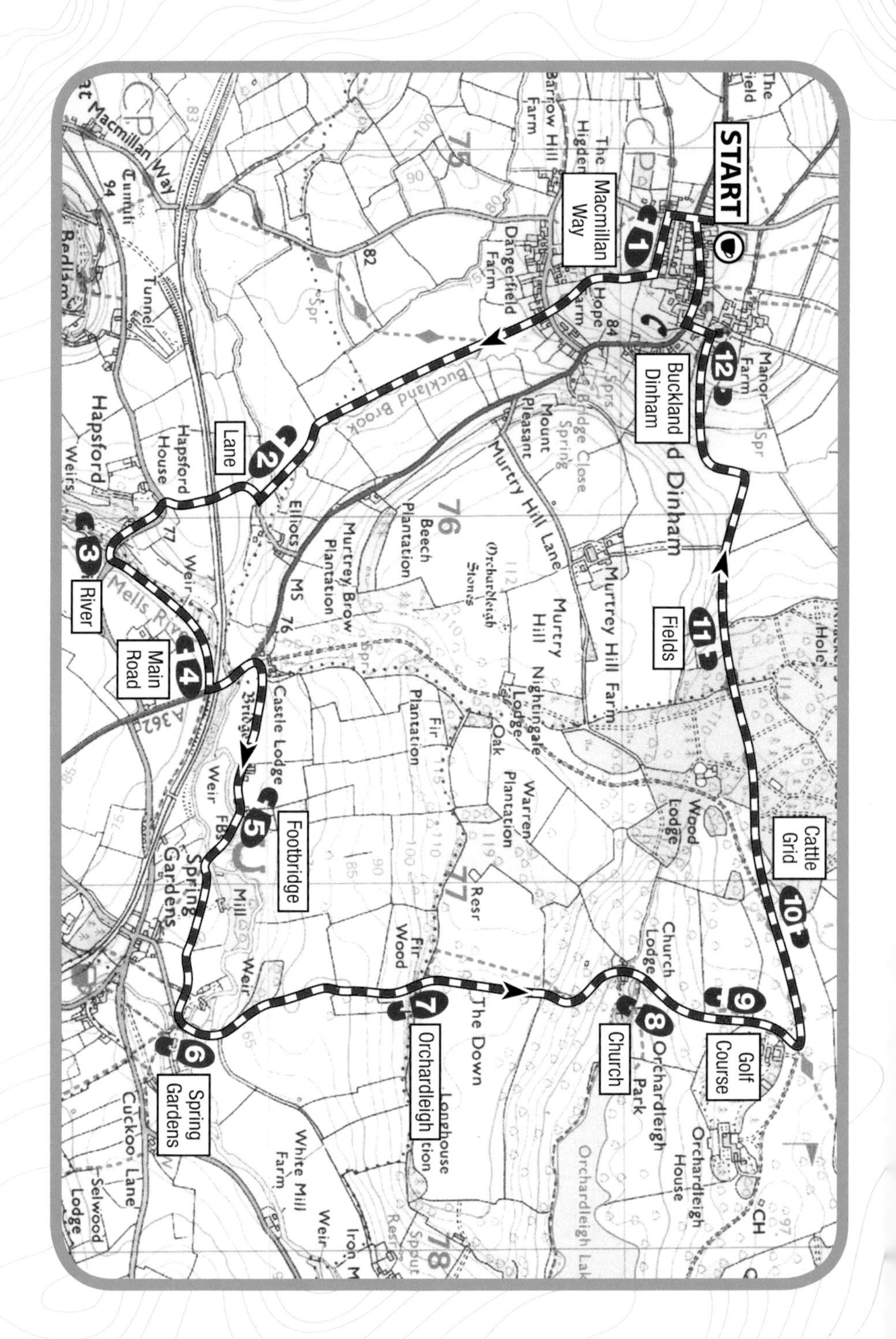
START
Macmillan Way
1
Lane
2
River
3
Main Road
4
Footbridge
5
Spring Gardens
6
Orchardleigh
7
Church
8
Golf Course
9
Cattle Grid
10
Fields
11
Buckland Dinham
12
Buckland Brook
Mells River
Murtry Hill Lane
Hapsford
Orchardleigh Park
The Down
A362

Buckland Dinham walk

A walk that explores one of the largest estates and parkland in the Mendip area, north of Frome, at Orchardleigh. It starts high, so there are great views across the country in East Mendip and then criss-crosses several times the once very bustling Mells River - an area abounding in derelict and some converted mills - before entering Orchardleigh estate and visiting a special little church on a lake. It's easy walking with a couple of very modest hills, but there are several stiles. Mainly the going should be good underfoot.

MAP: OS Explorer 142 Shepton Mallet & Mendip Hills East

GRID REF: 753 512

DISTANCE: 5.1 miles

TIME: About 3 hours walking

PARK: In the village of Buckland Dinham on the A362 Radstock – Frome road. Go to The Bell Inn, the very friendly c16th pub on the western end of the village in the conservation area. The landlord has given permission for walkers to park – tucked away in the car park behind the pub.

Orchardleigh parkland

START: Cross the main road and go down Sands Cross Lane. Take the first footpath left over a stile onto a path between fences.

1 MACMILLAN WAY

At the end, bend right into a field. Here we join the Macmillan Way.

This long distance path was set up to help the well known cancer charity by donations from sponsored walks and the sale of publications. It stretches some 209 miles from Lincolnshire into Dorset.

You get good views ahead over the valley. Keep straight on and cross a well worn stone slab stile.

Continue on, take a stile left and carry on down. Cross a stile onto a lane.

Go on, over the stile opposite and on through a field. Soon leave the Macmillan Way which bears right. Carry on through fields, over stiles, following the Buckland Brook. Eventually come out over a stile onto a small lane.

2 LANE

After turning right, soon cross the main railway line to a larger road. Cross with care to the wall opposite and turn left down a footpath alongside the wall. This drops down to Hapsford and the site of one of many old mills along the Mells River.

Rivers were one of the great sources of power before and during the Industrial Revolution. Rivers such as the Mells provided power to turn machinery that not only made flour for bread, but also turned iron into sharp edged cutting tools that forged an empire.

3 RIVER

Cross the river, go up and take the first footpath left by a lay-by and this takes you along the river. Reach an interesting area by an extended stone bridge.

River Mells

It is worth going to the river's edge here by the remains of an old weir – perhaps once an important mill.

Carry on along the footpath, noticing what looks like the remains of an old canal on your right.

Pass an iron rail bridge, go through a kissing gate and turn up right to reach the busy A362.

MAIN ROAD

Cross with great care and turn left over the Mells River again and soon reach the entrance to Orchardleigh Park.

Before the entrance, turn right by a lodge through a large gate and follow the drive/track to a riding establishment. At the end, go right over a footbridge.

FOOTBRIDGE

Once over, go across the field to a stile on the far side. Cross this and a bridge over the river. Here is another old weir serving a mill. Bear left on the path coming close to the hedge left (don't go straight across the field). Soon cross a drive leading to a mill. Keep on, bearing slightly right across the field to another stile. Then it is straight on along the hedge. Reach a drive to yet another huge old mill and go ahead over a stile and across a small field to the lane at Spring Gardens.

SPRING GARDENS

Turn left. Stay on this, crossing the river once again and ignoring a side path. Start to climb and at the end, join the public footpath which continues on. A stile takes you up through a small wooded area. Continue to climb and on the top see Orchardleigh House ahead.

The old Orchardleigh House was just south of the church but was demolished. The present one was built in 1856 by Thomas Henry Wyatt for William Duckworth. The estate was sold in 1986 after the death of Arthur Duckworth and work began on a grand redevelopment, but was halted for 13 years after financial problems and was restarted in 2002. It is now a top class hotel and prime wedding venue with several converted houses as well as a golf course.

The wall and ditch to your left are somewhat overgrown and worn down, but in their heyday were a sight to behold! No cluttering up the landscape with fences, the 'ha ha' took the ancient system of Iron Age hill fort defence (the ditch and stone faced bank) and turned it into effective stockproofing where animals would find it difficult to cross. So called a 'ha ha' because of the exclamation some would make in surprise at discovering it.

➤ Come into the Orchardleigh estate.

This is a wonderful example of how our landscape is constantly changing as our requirements of it vary. The parkland is no longer needed to provide grazing for wild deer that also provided food in the Middle Ages; neither is it used as a great ride and extension of the pleasure gardens by those of the c18th and c19th. Now it is a golf course and hotel in the grandest of settings. Big estates today are big business.

ORCHARDLEIGH

Follow the fenced path, cross an airstrip, and continue on the fenced path. You get a fine view of Orchardleigh Lake and can also see right the White Horse above Westbury, Wiltshire.

CHURCH

Join a track to go downhill. On the right is the beautiful little c13th church of St Mary's, Orchardleigh, in a unique setting at the edge of a lake with a moat around the church.

So, it is often referred to as 'the church on the island.' Its remoteness means there is no electricity and all the services are candlelit, with an organ that has to be pumped by hand! The churchyard contains the grave of the poet Sir Henry Newbolt. It is a favourite church for weddings with receptions held at Orchardleigh House.

GOLF COURSE

Continue up the drive which takes you uphill and across the golf course. Ignore side turns

Orchardleigh church

and continue to a junction with the main drive. Here you rejoin the Macmillan Way.

(If you want to have a look at Orchardleigh House, make a detour right of a couple of minutes).

To continue our circle, follow the drive left. There will be some traffic for the golf clubhouse which is beyond Orchardleigh House.

The village lock-up

CATTLE GRID

Cross the cattle grid and fork right away from the drive across the grass between large oaks. You should pass a waymark arrow on an oak tree. Continue on into a woodland conservation area and join a path.

Cross a track with buildings over left and maintain direction in the woods.

Just before a bend, leave the track and take a more indistinct track straight on. Shortly look for the Macmillan Way sign on a tree.

FIELDS

Cross a stile into a field. Go straight down the right edge. Cross a stile by a gate. Do a dog leg, going left a couple of yards, then right again, heading for Buckland Dinham and church above. Follow the field edge, go left in the corner and a short way along go right on a small path and cross a footbridge. Go straight up the field towards the church, then follow a path on to the church of St Michael and All Angels.

BUCKLAND DINHAM

Opposite is the village lock up.

Here you could be incarcerated for various wrong-doings such as drunkenness, by the village officials.

Turn left past the lock-up to the main road. Follow the pavement right through the village back to The Bell Inn.

The Bell Inn,
Buckland Dinham
01373 462956

Stoke St Michael walk

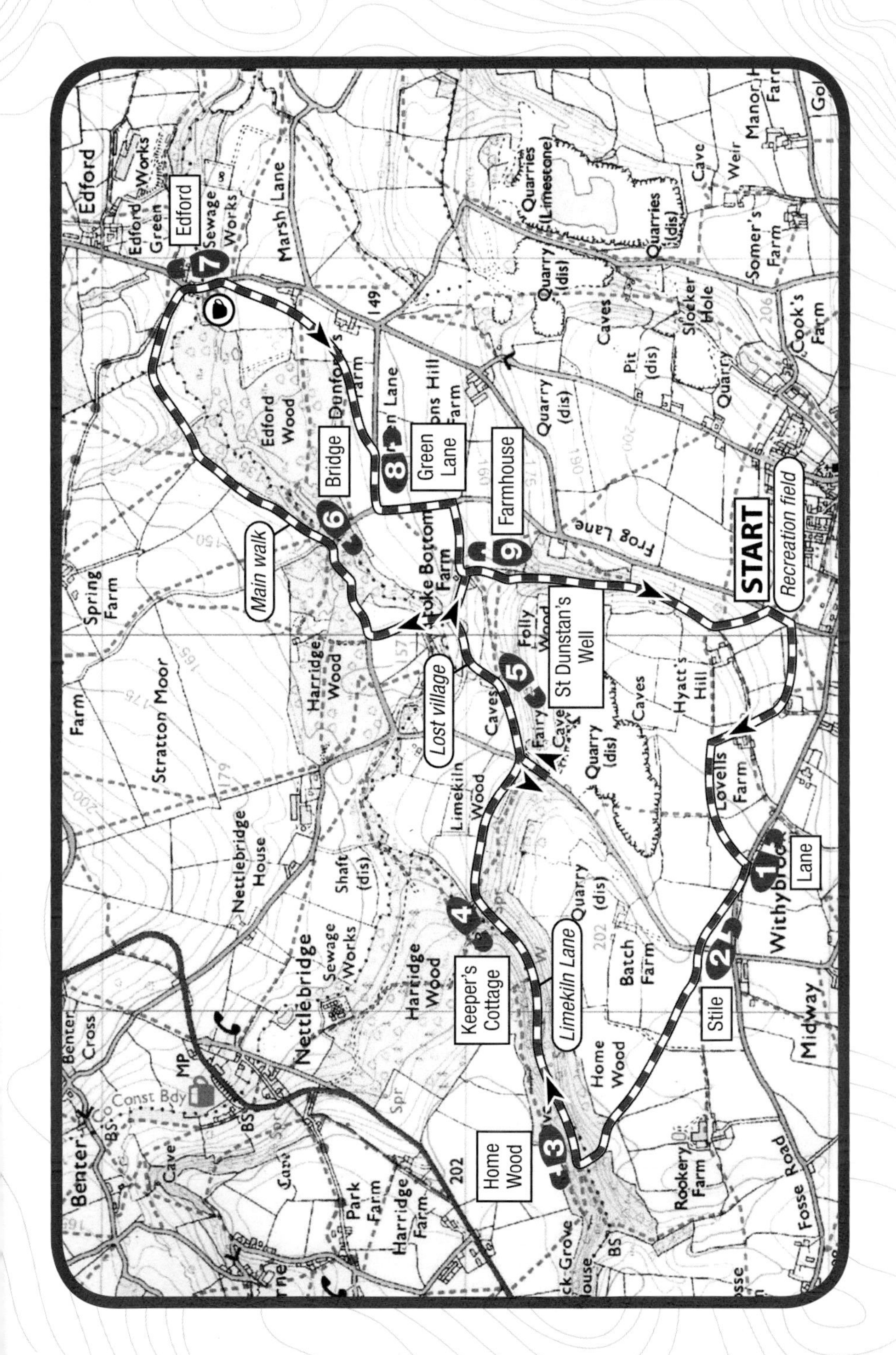

START
Recreation field
Edford
Bridge
Green Lane
Farmhouse
St Dunstan's Well
Lost village
Main walk
Keeper's Cottage
Limekiln Lane
Home Wood
Stile
Lane
Edford
Edford Green
Sewage Works
Marsh Lane
Edford Wood
Dunford's Farm
Stoke Bottom Farm
Folly Wood
Harridge Wood
Spring Farm
Stratton Moor
Nettlebridge House
Nettlebridge
Limekiln Wood
Fairy Cave
Caves
Quarry (dis)
Quarries (Limestone)
Quarries (dis)
Slocker Hole
Somer's Farm
Cook's Farm
Manor Farm
Weir
Cave
Frog Lane
Hyatt's Hill
Lovells Farm
Withybrook
Batch Farm
Midway
Rookery Farm
Fosse Road
Park Farm
Harridge Farm
Benter Cross
Benter
Co Const Bdy
Shaft (dis)

Stoke St Michael walk

Two walks in one! An attractive East Mendip circle through quiet countryside from Stoke St Michael finding a lost village and exploring the land of the great Mendip agricultural revolutionary, John Billingsley. Follow the woodland path he took to the old village alongside the Mells Stream in the once vibrant industrial area. Walk through Somerset Wildlife Trust woodland and water meadows. The full round goes along an old packhorse trail, along the line of the former canal and passes a great riverside pub. There are stiles but they should be ok for dogs. It's a great opportunity to see and hear birdlife.

MAP: OS Explorer 142 Shepton Mallet & Mendip Hills East

GRID REF: 660 471

DISTANCE: 4.6 miles or 2.75 miles

TIME: 2.5 or 1.5 hours walking

PARK: At the football/ recreation field on the edge of Stoke St Michael. The village is north east of Shepton Mallet, between Leigh-upon-Mendip and Oakhill. In the village turn west by the Knatchbull Arms towards Oakhill and then right on a small lane signed to Holcombe. The recreation area car park is on the right.

View across country

START: Ignore footpath opposite. Cross the road, turn left and shortly take the stile on the right in the hedge. Head across veering slightly left aiming for the right of a farmhouse and a protruding wall corner. Cross two stiles then out to a track. Go right down to a junction of tracks. Take the marked path straight on through a gate into a field up a rough track. Go over another stile and bear leftish towards double power poles and left, beyond the first 'hedge' of trees, along the field edge to a corner stile. Continue along a fence and wall, and through the gate in the corner onto a small lane.

LANE

Turn right for about a minute, and opposite a cottage, cross the stile hidden in the hedge right. Then go diagonally across the field towards the first power pole, on through a metal gate about halfway along the edge. Cross the stone stile onto a lane – it's quite steep.

STILE

Go over a splendid stepped stone stile on the other side.

Choose the footpath towards Home Wood following the right edge of the field. Go over a track and stiles to continue along the right edge.

Stepped stone stile

Just before the field drops, go right over another stone stile.

HOME WOOD

Follow the path down into Home Wood, into a cool shaded atmospheric area of mosses and ferns. Cross the footbridge and go up to reach crossing Limekiln Lane.

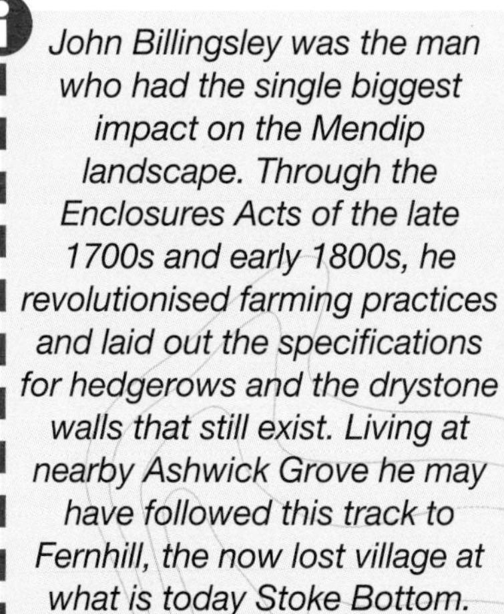

John Billingsley was the man who had the single biggest impact on the Mendip landscape. Through the Enclosures Acts of the late 1700s and early 1800s, he revolutionised farming practices and laid out the specifications for hedgerows and the drystone walls that still exist. Living at nearby Ashwick Grove he may have followed this track to Fernhill, the now lost village at what is today Stoke Bottom.

Go right along the Mells Stream. Pass one or two huge overhanging craggy boulders. ➤

See remains of work along the stream – leats, weirs, sluices, would all have been in place to provide power for mills and machinery. These works include 'lion cages', the work of Billingsley who 'captured' the water along the way to feed water meadows below.

Notice how the stream is gaining strength as we proceed through Harridge Wood (in the care of Somerset Wildlife Trust).

KEEPER'S COTTAGE

At the track end reach Keeper's Cottage, a former gamekeeper's cottage and now a prime bat habitat. Enter the water meadows through a kissing gate and maintain direction with woodland on the right. Eventually reach a lane.

One of the 'lion cages'

For a quick look at Fairy Cave quarry, turn up right for a minute and look through the gate on the left. It is disused and not generally open to the public but there is access for climbers and cavers. This limestone quarry was operating from the 1920s until 1977. The area is rich in beautifully decorated caves and underground water systems. Fairy Cave is rated amongst the top 20 caves in the country for its content.

Return to the footpath, cross the lane and go through a gate. Follow the path on below the hill.

ST DUNSTAN'S WELL

Reach St Dunstan's Well, a Site of Special Scientific Interest and once thought to be a holy well. A great spring of water rushes out under a rock (now caged), from an underground river which begins in an adjoining valley.

Formerly known as Stoke St Michael Slocker, it contains an important cave system including a series of spectacular naturally decorated caves in four miles of mapped passage.

Take the permissive path between the stone pillars (not the footpath into the field) and this leads you on by the water to remains of the bustling village of Fernhill.

There is not much to see other than the ruins of a paper mill with a fast flowing stepped weir and further along some evidence of the former Stoke House. In Spring, there are abundant snowdrops – perhaps a legacy from the former occupation. Fernhill once boasted a logwood mill and paper mill in a hamlet of about 40 houses with a population of about 200. There was a grand mansion, Stoke House, with splendid staircases, an Adam fireplace, stables, lawns and pleasure gardens and pastures and woods. From 1778 it was the home of the Chichester family but was abandoned by the late 1920s. Later it was dismantled piecemeal for its stone to be used in other buildings. Parts of the cellars still remain. The paper mill and cottages were abandoned much earlier, certainly by 1841.

Continue and join the drive to Stoke Bottom Farm.

For the short route: Turn right to the whitewashed farmhouse and follow from '9.FARMHOUSE'.
For the full route: Turn left up the drive, crossing the stream, passing a modern day Stoke House to a lane at the top.

The old packhorse bridge

6 BRIDGE

Follow it right for a few minutes to a left hand bend just before a bridge.

Take the footpath left through a wooden kissing gate before the bridge, soon coming into a field. Follow the field edge with Edford Wood – another Somerset Wildlife sanctuary - on your right.

This like other woods in the area was once worked for coal, before the c18th and there is hummocky evidence of bell pits and spoil heaps.

Keep on, going through a kissing gate and later over a piped metal stile. Cross a small side stream and enter a field. Proceed down the centre and soon see ahead the old packhorse bridge.

It was the first bridge constructed over the ill-fated Dorset and Somerset Canal. The packhorse trail linked the coal pits on Stratton Common down here to Edford. The Dorset and Somerset Canal was one of many failed attempts to link the Bristol Channel to the English Channel with an inland waterway system. Established by Act in 1796, an 11 mile branch of this canal ran from Frome to Nettlebridge to transport coal. But capital ran out. Canals put the packhorse out of business, then the canals lost out to the railways!

Go up steps and turn right over the bridge.

EDFORD

Follow the old packhorse route to the main road in the hamlet of Edford which is part of Holcombe. Opposite is the welcoming Duke of Cumberland pub with a pretty garden by the river.

Go right (or left if coming from the pub) up the road for a short way. Find a stile on the right by a gate. Go up the rough field to a barrier stile along the top hedge with a farm left. Then cross the narrow field, go over a stile and bear diagonally right across to the far corner with a gap between hedge and wood. A gate leads into a large field. Head diagonally down aiming to the right of trees along the far left edge, about three quarters of the way along. There is a gate and stile and a rather overgrown few yards to reach Green Lane (not marked).

GREEN LANE

Turn right, dropping, and take the first left climbing gently. After a few minutes turn right on the grassy bridleway leading to Stoke Bottom Farm. Pass sheds and drop down to the whitewashed farmhouse.

FARMHOUSE

(The shorter route joins here). Pass down the left side of the farmhouse and through a marked metal gate. Then head across to the wooded valley and a stile. (Ignore a path and stile on the left as you enter the wood). The first part of the path can be difficult with fallen trees and you may need a small dog-leg to get to a stile further on. But soon flow into a much better and well used path/track.

Further on, pass a new low house up right and cross its drive. Continue on over another stile. Enter a field soon and maintain direction for a couple of minutes. Look for the remains of a small quarry right. At this point, with a large gate visible ahead, bear up left (not signed) to the lane above and the parking area opposite.

The Duke of Cumberland
01761 233731

Shepton Mallet
walk

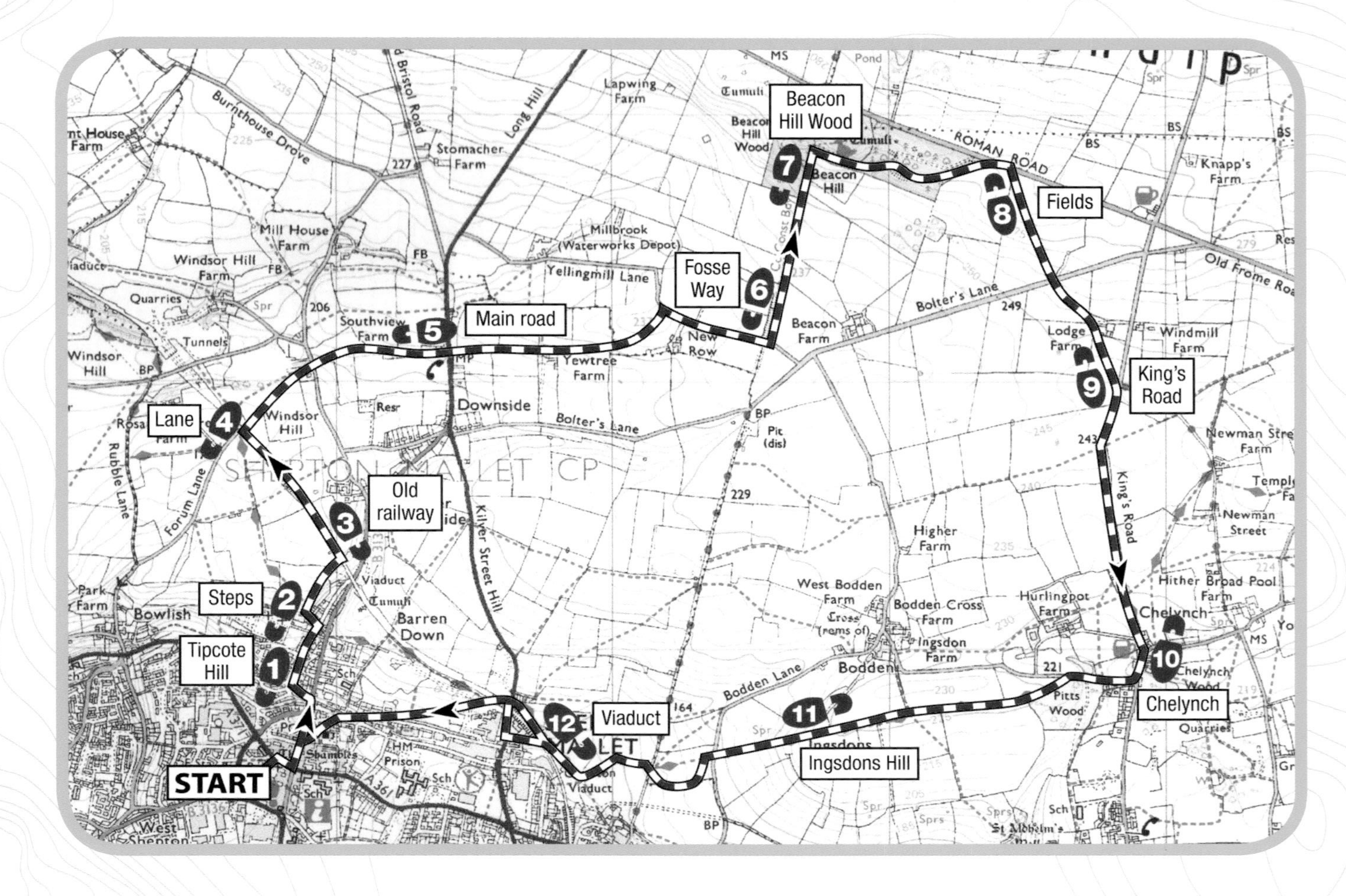
START
Tipcote Hill
Steps
Old railway
Lane
Main road
Fosse Way
Beacon Hill Wood
Fields
King's Road
Chelynch
Ingsdons Hill
Viaduct

Shepton Mallet walk

Throughout this walk in East Mendip tread in the footsteps of the ancients, from the Roman soldier on the Fosse Way to the shepherd moving his flocks on the hill. The circle harks back to former transport - the old railway - and even earlier than that, the Roman Fosse Way. It weaves through the historic part of the ancient wool town of Shepton Mallet and out along the old railway before cutting across country. Visit an ancient wood - especially beautiful in bluebell time - pass a welcoming pub and then go across and down to a viaduct and up through the old town again. You could stop off at a garden, café and shopping outlet. There are several stiles and no major hills.

MAP: OS Explorer 142 Shepton Mallet & Mendip Hills East

GRID REF: 527 435

DISTANCE: 7.75 miles

TIME: About 4-4.5 hours walking

PARK: In the Commercial Road car park in the centre of Shepton. £3.60 for 4 hours plus. Park at the back of the car park near the toilets.

Down Tipcote Hill

START: Leave the car park at the back alongside the toilets. At the road, turn right, cross and at traffic lights turn left on the pedestrianised High Street into the old shambles with the 500 year old market cross

This has seen a Civil War skirmish and the hanging of Monmouth rebels.

Go on down to the end. Cross the main road and after a few yards go down steps left on Tipcote Hill.

TIPCOTE HILL

At a junction, turn right in the main street (not Longbridge). Soon pass historic c14th Longbridge House on the right.

JAMES
DUKE OF MONMOUTH
STAYED IN
LONGBRIDGE HOUSE
BEFORE HIS DEFEAT AT THE
BATTLE OF SEDGEMOOR
JULY 1685

It is best known for being where the Duke of Monmouth stayed before and after the Battle of Sedgemoor in 1685, before he was later executed for treason. The house is also locally famous for being where John Lewis (of John Lewis Partnership fame) lived for much of his childhood. In more recent years the house has been owned by the Bishop of London.

Go straight over a small roundabout and continue on up with the massive viaduct up ahead. Go up under a stone arch and a few yards past this follow the footpath up left signed to Maesbury. Climb to the top and turn right up steps

STEPS

After a kissing gate take the right path up. Leave steps, fork up right and go through another kissing gate to follow the right edge of the field onto the top.

Stay along the right edge, cross a stone stile and keep on the footpath. Leave the field and reach the end of the viaduct and the old railway line.

This was part of the Somerset, and Dorset line which was also affectionately known as 'The Slow and Dirty' after the initials, S&D.

OLD RAILWAY

Turn left along the old line and under a metal bridge all the way to a quiet lane.

LANE

Follow the lane right to a junction. Cross to the stile opposite and go along the right edge of the field. Cross a stile and maintain direction in the next field. The footpath arrow takes you into derelict and atmospheric Southview Farm.

This is almost a 'monument' to those who worked this land, shaped the fields and raised the crops and animals. What hopes, dreams, sad moments and joyous occasions there must have been here.

Go through on the track to the busy A37.

MAIN ROAD

On your left on the main road is the former old coaching inn, the Downside Inn.

Cross the road to follow the marked footpath ahead over a stile and keep to the left of the field. Cross a ladder stile and keep on in the next field. To the right, on a low ridge, you can see a modern solar farm. Near the end, go left into the field at the side and immediately right over a stile to continue as before, and pass a farm right. Cross a rather awkward combination of two stiles separated by a slab stile.

This 'triple stile' has been erected to protect the old slab stile from the cattle that will be grazing here and do have a habit of clambering over these old slab stiles to go visiting in the next field!

Maintain direction. Pass a large cattle trough made from an old industrial boiler. There's another stone stile after which, go left across the field. Up ahead in the distance is ancient Beacon Wood with round barrows in the field to the left of it. Go under the power line to the far side. Cross onto a lane and turn right for a few minutes. Just before a bend, turn

stone stile

left on a byway - the old Fosse Way, by boulders which prevent vehicle access.

FOSSE WAY

Notice one section of the Way which is raised with ditches on each side.

Could these ditches be the same as those that would have run at the edge of the Roman road? Such ditches were designed to take the water run off from the raised section of the road called the 'aggar'. The Fosse Way, named from the Latin word 'Fossa' for ditch, ran from Exeter to Lincoln, a total of over 370 miles.

BEACON HILL WOOD

Enter the wood, maintained by the Woodland Trust. Pass a stone boundary marker with a well-sited bench. Further on at a second boundary marker, leave the track and go straight ahead climbing. Shortly bend right on a path which runs below the wood with open fields and good views to the right. It is all open access. There should be beautiful bluebells in season.

Beacon Hill Wood takes its name from the fire Beacon that used to stand on a hillock within what is now the wood when this was all open heathland. This was an Elizabethan early warning system across the country to be used for various purposes including the sighting of the Spanish Armada.

Bend left on the track up into the wood. After a few paces, turn right on the crossing path and simply follow this along the top. It bears left and reaches the main road near the wood end.

Turn right along the edge for 2-3 minutes. Before the road rises, cross a stile on the right (opposite a large field gate).

FIELDS

Diagonally cross the field, getting widespread views over the Somerset Levels and Glastonbury Tor as well as to Cranmore Tower on the left. Head to the right of a clump of trees and down to the stile in the bottom left corner onto a road. Take the footpath more or less opposite over a stone stile into

another field. Head across towards the farm to cross a stile in the bottom corner. Follow a short stretch of fencing, cross a stile, track and another stile and head across the field to a field gate half way along the far edge.

KING'S ROAD

A stile brings you onto King's Road. Turn right and after about 0.6 of a mile reach the hamlet of Chelynch and the welcoming Poacher's Pocket. We have now joined the East Mendip Way (EMW).

The East Mendip Way was created to complement the West Mendip Way (WMW), set up to celebrate the Queen's Silver Jubilee,1977. It runs from Wells to Frome

CHELYNCH

Go past the pub and take the first lane right towards Bodden. Pass a pond right, and at the end of woodland on the left, go left on the EMW into a field. Follow the left edge, go into another field and maintain direction. In the corner reach a track and follow it on. Ahead is Glastonbury Tor. Go through a squeeze stile.

These are forms of stile commonly used where footpaths cross dry stone walls in England.

INGSDONS HILL

Follow the hedge on your right on to Ingsdons Hill looking down onto Shepton Mallet. Keep on following the East Mendip Way, descending. After a kissing gate continue down to a lane with the hedge left. Go across to an old orchard. The footpath should go straight through but now seems to bend left through the orchard to a field. Then turn right down the orchard edge and keep on across the field to a stone stile. You are back on the Fosse Way.

Go over another slab stile. Pick your way across the field towards the viaduct, aiming for the third arch to the left of the vertical downpipe. (If this is ploughed or difficult to cross, go round the left edge). Cross a stile and go right. On the other side of the wall on your left is Kilver Court Gardens originally created by the Showering Brothers of 'Babycham' fame back in the 1960s and recently revived.

VIADUCT

Go under Charlton viaduct.

It was originally built to take the Somerset and Dorset Railway across the valley. It is the longest (328 yards) viaduct on the Somerset and Dorset Railway route and towers 49ft above the Sheppey River.

Continue out to the main road with the old Showerings factory opposite.

Turn right, for about 100 yards past the Mulberry Factory Shop and Designer Village. Here also is a chance to visit Kilver Court Gardens and cafés.

Cross the road, turn right and just past the old railway bridge turn left up steps. The path goes under the old line and then turns right at the back of the factory. Continue for several minutes between fence and wall. At a gate, turn left towards the town along a field edge and then on down a tarmac path between walls, past a school.

See ahead the amazing tower of c12th St Peter and St Paul's church. Before the end, turn right through a wall by a Mendip 40 sign - the original name for the East Mendip Way. Cross the mill stream on a bridge from where you can look left to see the entrance of the old prison.

Dating from 1610, it housed French POWs during the Napoleonic War, and was an American Military Prison during WW2. The Domesday book, a copy of Magna Carta and the logs of HMS Victory were all housed here for safety during that time.

Continue on and up steps. Cross a road to go up Peter's Street opposite. Reach the church.

Architectural historian Nikolaus Pevsner described the roof as "the finest 15th century carved oak wagon-roof in England"

Turn right round the church and then right back to the market cross. Turn up left, retracing your steps to the start.

The Poacher's Pocket, Chelynch **01749 880220**

Cafés at Kilver Court **01749 340363**